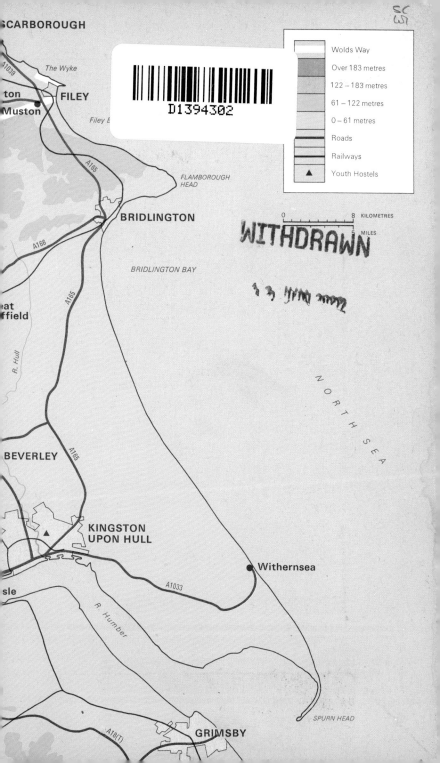

SCARBOROUGH

The Wyke

ton
Muston

FILEY

Filey B

A1039

SC
ω5

	Wolds Way
	Over 183 metres
	122 – 183 metres
	61 – 122 metres
	0 – 61 metres
	Roads
	Railways
▲	Youth Hostels

A165

FLAMBOROUGH
HEAD

A166

BRIDLINGTON

0   8 KILOMETRES

5 MILES

WITHDRAWN

BRIDLINGTON BAY

A165

at
ffield

R. Hull

N
O
R
T
H

S
E
A

BEVERLEY

A165

KINGSTON
UPON HULL

▲

sle

Withernsea

A1033

R. Humber

SPURN HEAD

A18(T)

GRIMSBY

Key to cover illustration:
1: Fieldfare   2: Redwing   3: Curlew   4: Partridges   5: Pheasants
6: Fox   7: Hawthorn

The Wolds Way

Roger Ratcliffe

F

Long-distance footpath guide No 12

London: Her Majesty's Stationery Office 1982

Published by the Countryside Commission

Cover:
From Settrington Beacon, looking towards the North York Moors

Pages x-xi Looking north from Staxton Wold

The maps in this guide are extracts from Ordnance Survey 1:25,000 maps sheet nos SE 82/92, 83/93, 84, 85, 86, 87, 97, TA 02/12, 07/17, 08.

Drawings:
Louis Mackay

Photographs:
Simon Warner

Long-distance footpath guides published for the Countryside Commission by HMSO:

The Pennine Way, by Tom Stephenson: 120 pages, £3.95 net
The Cleveland Way, by Alan Falconer: 144 pages, £3.95 net
The Pembrokeshire Coast Path, by John H Barrett: 124 pages, £3.95 net
Offa's Dyke Path, by John B Jones: 124 pages, £3.95 net
Cornwall Coast Path, by Edward C Pyatt: 120 pages £3.95 net
The Ridgeway Path, by Seán Jennett: 120 pages, £3.95 net
South Downs Way, by Seán Jennett: 112 pages, £3.95 net
Dorset Coast Path, by Brian Jackman: 122 pages, £3.95 net
South Devon Coast Path, by Brian Le Messurier: 122 pages, £3.95 net
Somerset and North Devon Coast Path, by Clive Gunnell: 112 pages, £3.95 net
The North Downs Way, by Denis Herbstein: 148 pages, £3.95 net

Government Bookshops:
49 High Holborn, London WC1V 6HB
13a Castle Street, Edinburgh EH2 3AR
41 The Hayes, Cardiff CF1 1JW
Brazennose Street, Manchester M60 8AS
Southey House, Wine Street, Bristol BS1 2BQ
258 Broad Street, Birmingham B1 2HE
80 Chichester Street, Belfast BT1 4JY

Government publications are also available through booksellers

Prepared for the Countryside Commission by the Central Office of Information

Countryside Commission, John Dower House, Crescent Place, Cheltenham, Glos. GL50 3RA

The waymark sign is used in plaque or stencil form by the Countryside Commission on long-distance footpaths

Printed in England for Her Majesty's Stationery Office by
Linneys of Mansfield

ISBN 0 11 700899 0   Dd 696402   C250

Contents

Maps of route

Maps reference

Not necessarily rights of way

M I or A 6(M)   Motorway

A 31(T)   Trunk road

A 35   Main road

B 3074   Secondary road

A 35   Dual carriageway

Narrow roads with passing places are annotated

Unfenced roads and tracks are shown by pecked lines

Road generally more than 4·3m wide

Road generally less than 4·3m wide

Road generally less than 4·3m wide, untarred

Other road, drive or track

Path

RAILWAYS

Multiple track | Standard gauge

Single track

Narrow gauge

Siding

Cutting

Embankment

Tunnel

Road over & under

Level crossing, station

PUBLIC RIGHTS OF WAY

Public paths { Footpath / Bridleway }

Road used as a public path

DANGER AREA — MOD ranges in the area
Danger! Observe warning notices

Public rights of way indicated by these symbols have been derived from Definitive Maps as amended by later enactments or instruments held by Ordnance Survey and are shown subject to the limitations imposed by the scale of mapping
The representation on this map of any other road, track or path is no evidence of the existence of a right of way

BOUNDARIES

Geographical County

Administrative County, County Borough or County of City

London Borough

Municipal Borough, Urban or Rural District, Burgh or District Council

Civil Parish*

Borough, Burgh or County Constituency

Coincident boundaries are shown by the first appropriate symbol opposite

*Shown alternately when coincident with other boundaries

SYMBOLS

Church or chapel { with tower / with spire / without tower or spire }

Glasshouse, Youth hostel

Bus or coach station

Lighthouse, lightship, beacon

Triangulation station

Triangulation point on { church, chapel, lighthouse, beacon, building & chimney }

°BP, BS   Boundary Post, Stone

·T, A, R   Telephone, public, AA, RAC

P. · MP, MS   Post office, Mile Post, Stone

VILLA   Roman antiquity (AD 43 to AD 420)

Castle   Other antiquities

Site of antiquity

⚔ 1066   Site of battle (with date)

Gravel, sand pit

Disused pit or quarry

Chalk pit, clay pit or quarry

Refuse or slag heap

Sloping masonry

· W, Spr   Well, Spring

Water

Sand, sand & shingle

Mud

Dunes

NT   National Trust always open

NT   National Trust opening restricted

NTS   NTS   National Trust for Scotland

Electricity transmission line

pylon   pole

VEGETATION

Coniferous trees

Non-coniferous trees

Coppice

Orchard

Scrub

Bracken, rough grassland

In some areas bracken (∴) and rough grassland (⋯⋯) are shown separately

Heath

Shown collectively as rough grassland on some sheets

Reeds

Marsh

Saltings

50·	Determined	ground survey
285 ·	by	air survey

Vertical face

Loose rock · Boulders · Outcrop · Scree

75
60
50

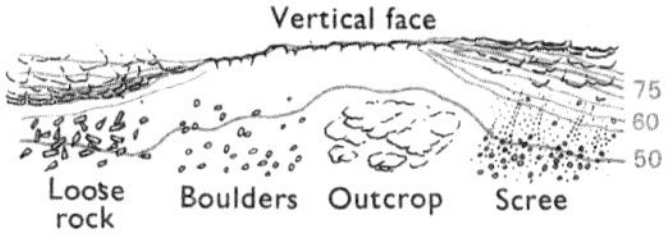

Contours are at 5 metre vertical interval

urface heights are to the nearest metre bove mean sea level. Heights shown close o a triangulation pillar refer to the station eight at ground level and not necessarily o the summit

The symbols shown below appear on first series OS maps which are used on maps 10 to 17 and 21, and part of maps 9, 18 and 20.

Footpaths		FP Fenced	FP Unfenced

Public Buildings

Glasshouses

Quarry & Gravel Pit

Orchard

National Trust Area — Sheen Common NT

Furze

„ „ „ Scotland — NTS

Rough Pasture
Heath & Moor

Osier Bed

Marsh

Reeds

Well

Park, Fenced

Spring — Spᵍ o

Wind Pump — Wd Pp .

Wood, Coniferous, Fenced

Wood, Non-Coniferous Unfenced

Contours are at 25 feet vertical interval.

Brushwood, Fenced & Unfenced

Spot Height — 123 ·

Ferries
Foot   Vehicle

Sand Hills

Mud

Flat Rock

HWMOT

Slopes

HWMMT

Δ Beacon

Lake

Sand

Lightship

Bridge

Highest point to which Medium Tides flow

Sand & Shingle

Canal

Aqueduct

Lock

Weir

Cliff

Towing   Path

Ford

FB (Footbridge)

Lighthouse

Dam

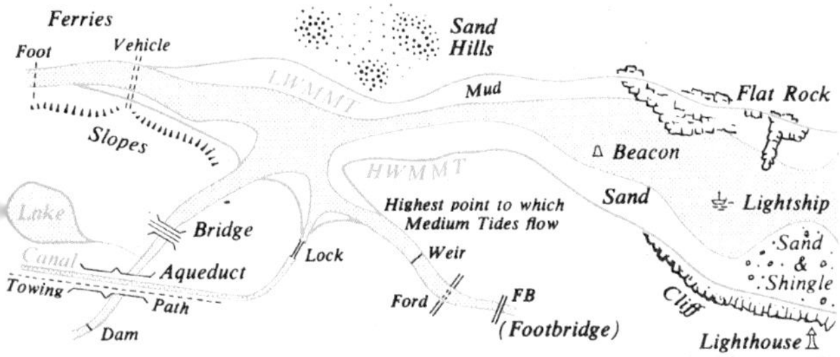

WOLDS WAY

TEMPORARY ROUTE   • • • • • • • • • • • • • • PROPOSED ROUTE

Because some short parts of the route had not been formally agreed when this book went to press, some sections of temporary route are shown on the maps. The Countryside Commission hopes they will not be in use for very long. Always follow the waymarking.

The opening of the Wolds Way is a triumph of common sense and co-operation between the farmers and landowners along it and those who planned the route. It has taken only five years since the Secretary of State for the Environment approved the line of the route to negotiate the 17 kilometres of new rights of way needed to complete the Way. Compare that with the 14 years it took to reach a stage when the first long-distance path, the Pennine Way, could be opened, albeit incomplete.

This is the first long-distance path to go almost entirely through agricultural land. In this way it is different from the 11 long-distance paths that had previously been designated, and which are being well used. Those, in the main, cross

downland, moorland, woodland, coastal cliffs, seashore. Here, on every side, modern farming practice can be seen at work – it is up to all future walkers of the Wolds Way to show that walking can co-exist peacefully with modern agriculture.

This guide-book is published to coincide with the opening of the Wolds Way on 2 October 1982. Another first – and full tribute should be paid to Roger Ratcliffe who bravely attempted to follow non-existent and overgrown paths to describe them for future walkers of the Way. I hope you will agree that the result is a splendid combination of detailed description and fascinating back-ground information that will encourage old faithfuls of the Wolds and newcomers alike to set out on this path with great anticipation.

Derek Barber
Chairman CC

Introduction

The Yorkshire Wolds surface unspectacularly from the Humber's gritty brown waters and adhesive mudbanks. As the sinuous waves of chalk roll gently northwards and then to the east, they form an increasingly beautiful and individual landscape, ending with a masterstroke of scenic grandeur – the gleaming cliffs of Flamborough and Bempton and the wide bay dominated by the dramatic rocky promontory of Filey Brigg.

With such a progressive heightening of visual appeal it is natural that the Wolds Way should begin on the flat Humber shore. Anyone standing at this point will find little that hints at the delights that follow on the 127-kilometre path to Filey cliffs. The landscape does not hit you between the eyes from a distance, as it does in the North York Moors, the Yorkshire Dales and the Lake District. The Wolds have, therefore, been mostly overlooked in the expansion of interest in rambling during the last 30 years.

But local ramblers have for years appreciated the charming countryside on their own doorstep. These were beauties that you had to discover entirely on foot. And when the Pennine Way was opened in 1965, they began thinking about a footpath that would link all the best features of their beloved Wolds. The walker and writer, A. J. Brown, as long ago as 1932, referred to 'the Wolds way' in a book about rambling in Yorkshire. At that time he was commending a walk in the general Wolds area; the idea of a continuous footpath came 35 years later.

The scope for an interesting long-distance route was enormous. It would stretch from the mighty Humber, right up the crescent-shaped Wolds, taking in dry valleys, peaceful villages, airy tops with sweeping views, and terminating at the finest bay on the east coast of England.

The Ramblers' Association first approached the National Parks Commission (soon to become the Countryside Commission) in 1967 and in the following year the idea was approved in principle both by the Commission and the East Riding County Council. It was in fact entirely an East Riding route, since the Cleveland Way, to which it was to be joined, ended abruptly at the North Riding boundary on the cliffs north of Filey. Local government reorganisation in 1974 did not alter

abbit Warren,
ear
illington

1

the start or finish of either route and the join remains as a relic of the old Yorkshire.

After five years of negotiation on the line of the route, a section near Londesborough was opened, on guaranteed rights of way including road lengths, by Lord Halifax as one of his later acts as Lord Lieutenant of the East Riding, in November 1973.

By 1975, after some alteration in the central section and with remaining conflicts on the line along much of the northern escarpment, the Commission felt ready to present a route for the Environment Secretary to see, and this was formally approved on 26 July 1977.

Since then there have been five major amendments to the route, including an extension to the Humber Bridge and Hessle Haven and the addition of an alternative section into Market Weighton. In Humberside, a meeting with farmers in the Newbald area finally brought about the transfer of the route on to a more easterly line to avoid unnecessary conflict with agriculture. In North Yorkshire the negotiation on the difficult northern section, where some 15 kilometres of entirely new rights of way had to be created, was carried through entirely without the use of compulsory powers, a triumph for reason and compromise in the context of this intensively farmed countryside.

With the opening of the footpath, there is now a continuous long-distance way of some 500 kilometres down the east of England. To the north of the Wolds Way runs the 150-kilometre-long Cleveland Way – between Helmsley, in the North York Moors, to the end of the Wolds Way near Filey. Across the walkway of the Humber Bridge begins the Viking Way (225 kilometres), which runs down the Lincolnshire Wolds and flat fens to end at Oakham, now in Leicestershire, but once the county town of the tiny extinct county of Rutland.

I first discovered the Wolds as a trainee journalist in Hull during the mid-1970s. I walked the Humber shore first and then spent many days on the coast from Flamborough to Filey. Later, I filled in the gaps and was charmed by Thixendale in particular. I did the bulk of the Wolds Way in one outing and genuinely regretted walking up Stocking Dale, knowing that this was the final stretch of chalk valley.

The research was made easier by the staff of the Countryside Commission's regional office in Leeds; Stephen Warburton, field officer of the Yorkshire Naturalists' Trust; the farmers I met along the way; and the staff of the local history section at Hull Central Library.

R.R.

Some advice

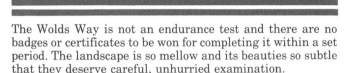

The Wolds Way is not an endurance test and there are no badges or certificates to be won for completing it within a set period. The landscape is so mellow and its beauties so subtle that they deserve careful, unhurried examination.

Whether you walk the footpath in several stages spread over a few weeks, months or even years, or in one almighty trek, depends on where you live and how much time you have. The main argument against doing it in bits and pieces is that unless you can persuade someone to chauffeur you around, dropping you off at one point and picking you up farther on, it is very difficult to do a stretch at a time, since there is little public transport.

Certainly, the 127-kilometre footpath (129 kilometres including South Cave and Sherburn) divides most easily into five different sections – as demonstrated by the following chapters which describe the route – but these are designed more for availability of beds than of buses.

Walkers of most ages can average at least three kilometres an hour and, allowing for stops to rest, inspect churches or other interesting features, peer at butterflies and admire views, each of the sections can be accomplished easily between breakfast and dinner.

For much of the footpath you need keep up nothing more than a gentle stroll. There are a few sections where the calf muscles will be tested, however – notably on the steep banks of Rabbit Warren and Nettle Dale near Millington and the climb up Deep Dale from Wintringham.

One difficulty you will not have, hopefully, is getting lost. So that disturbance to crops and livestock may be avoided, the local authorities have excelled themselves in waymarking the route. The path is also described in detail in this book, at points where confusion may arise. If in doubt, consult the map before stepping forward.

Waymarking
There are three kinds of signs and waymarks used on the Wolds Way. The one seen most often is the finger-post, an engraved wooden board used in the same way as a signpost. In Humberside it is morticed into a wooden post; in North Yorkshire it is bolted or screwed on to either metal or wood.

Footpath waymarks are used in both counties to show direction and status of path (footpath or bridleway).

Yellow arrows on a green background denote footpaths and blue arrows on yellow are for bridleways. The waymarks used are printed on to aluminium sheet and are durable as well as flexible enough to nail to curved surfaces.

The universal acorn symbol has been used in the form of the standard small plaque supplied by the Countryside Commission, as well as in stencil form. A combination of this symbol with the waymark arrow is a regular feature.

Buses and trains

In common with all rural areas, bus services in the Wolds are limited and their timetables favour villagers wishing to reach shopping towns like Driffield and Market Weighton rather than walkers wishing to find a bed or get back to their starting points. Details of what services there are can be obtained from the bus companies (addresses on page 109).

Many walkers from outside Yorkshire will get to the Wolds Way by train. There are frequent services to Hull from Doncaster, Leeds and York and the start of the footpath at Hessle is reached by train or bus from Hull, where the bus and railway stations are next to each other. At the other end, Filey is on a line to Hull and Scarborough, from where there are regular trains to York and Leeds.

There are bus services to some of the places of interest described at the end of the book, such as Malton, Pickering, Sledmere (bus from Fridaythorpe) and Skidby. Trains run from Filey to Bempton, Bridlington and Beverley.

What to take

Common sense will dictate what equipment and clothing you require for a long-distance walk. Clearly, your needs depend on the season you choose. In summer a lightweight anorak is better than the bulky heavyweight you wore across Helvellyn last Christmas. In cool weather, of course, it is better to be well wrapped up and to carry that obligatory spare sweater in your rucksack, preferably in a polythene bag in case water gets in. The essential qualities of winter clothing are that they are warm, windproof and waterproof.

Jeans are adequate but should be your last choice. The best option is corduroy, which dries out quite quickly. Shorts may be a good idea in summer, but be warned that the footpath is, in places, virtually overgrown with thorns and nettles in early summer.

An absolute essential at any time of the year is a pair of nylon rainproof over-trousers. These take up little room in a rucksack and need only be taken out for showers. They are often needed for morning walking when long grass is heavy with dew, or after even light rain as overhanging grass will soak your trousers in just a few yards.

The biggest decision you have to make on Wolds Way equipment is on the kind of footwear you should take. Most guides to rambling recommend the use of stout walking boots, well dubbined after each use and with Vibram soles for good grip. While these are certainly preferable, they are an expensive item for the occasional walker, and not essential for the Wolds Way. The alternative, which I used, is a pair of short, lightweight Wellingtons. They are available at most good outdoor shops. Their grip is as good as any Vibram sole and the fact that Hamish Brown, the Scottish mountaineer, swears by them is good enough for me.

Their value on the Wolds Way is that they do not feel like lead weights when mud clings to their soles, and they clean easily in a puddle, unlike leather walking boots. If you opt for Wellingtons, it is a good idea also to take along some padded plimsoles, of the type used for jogging. These I found to be a great relief for my feet when walking on the metalled road sections. As there are about 25 kilometres of road-walking, they are worth packing.

There is only one choice for inside boots or shoes and that is wool. Since you are giving your feet more punishment than they normally get, the more comfortable you make them, the fewer problems they will give. Soft woollen socks or stockings provide a good cushion. Make sure you put them on smoothly, and two pairs are better than one.

A good waterproof rucksack is essential – its size will depend on whether you are out just for a day or for a week. A large polythene bag is a good thing to add as a liner before packing, since there is nothing worse than finding that your change of clothing is wet. Keep daily necessities like snacks, drinks and maps at the top or in outer pockets.

Whatever you take, keep it to a minimum and remember that what feels easy to carry at the start of a walk can seem like a ton weight two days farther on. Try not to exceed 18 kilograms.

Whether you are bed-and-breakfasting or camping, be advised that there are few opportunities on the Wolds Way to buy food or fill up water-bottles. So make sure that you get your lunch or snack needs from kindly landladies at the start of the day.

Everything else you take is back to common sense. Musts are a watch, compass (although it is unlikely you will get lost), small first-aid kit, some spare energy-intensive food like mint cake, glucose tablets or barley sugar, and a torch and whistle for emergencies. The Ordnance Survey 1:50,000 maps required are sheet numbers 100, 101 and 106. It is hardly worth buying sheet 107, which has only the first few paces of the Wolds Way.

Wolds weather
The Yorkshire Wolds are, from a weather point of view, good walking country. That is to say, the rainfall is lower than in the Lake District and Pennines (the average is just 750 millimetres a year compared with an England and Wales

average of 912 millimetres). In the spring and early summer the area is swept by cool north-easterly winds which are good drying winds and pick up any lingering moisture from the land. And, in any case, puddles should clear fairly quickly by draining into the chalk.

Weather records pin-point the best period as early June. For a low rainfall at this time has coincided time and again with a quite astonishing peak on the sunshine graph. The records also show early to mid-August as a time of low sunshine and high rainfall, before late August provides another sunshine peak. Because of this, the cereals grown on the Wolds are harvested under the most favourable conditions and local farmers believe that they are blessed with some of the best growing weather in the country.

For the rest of the spring and summer, the well-known vagaries of the English weather take over and nothing is predictable. In winter, however, the Wolds suffer badly from snowdrifts, usually in January and February, and many of the high villages like Huggate and Warter and even Thixendale get snowed up.

Trying to forecast the weather in the Wolds is difficult. But one small tip is that for most of the year the prevailing wind is westerly; in the spring, however, this changes to a north-easterly.

On the coast, an interesting phenomenon is the sea 'fret' – a mist which often gathers a few kilometres offshore in a thick band spreading right across the horizon. This can come ashore without warning, and extreme care should be taken if you are walking on the cliff-tops north of Filey.

Staying friends with farmers
Virtually every step you take along the Wolds Way is on land that is someone's livelihood. Great care is needed, therefore,

Hereford bull

Charolais
bull

in making your presence as little felt as possible.

There are a few simple rules that should keep you on the right side of the farmer. The most important is to close gates behind you, although stiles have been provided beside gates for much of the Way. Also vital is to keep in single file along the sides of fields in which there are crops. And do not wander off the path. The farmer will not thank you for interfering with his livestock, crops or machinery – so leave them alone. And if you really must take a dog, then keep it on a lead at all times. The Wolds is a major sheep-rearing area and it is not always immediately apparent that there is a flock in the field you are crossing. Never light fires in farmers' fields and always be sure you have extinguished matches and cigarettes completely – grass and crop fires can so easily be started, especially at harvest time.

Remember, walkers are guests on farmland and many farmers and landowners have consented to new stretches of public footpath being created so that the Wolds Way can link together some of the finest countryside in the region. Do not let them down.

Bulls

In some places along the Wolds Way, farmers run bulls with their cattle which are being reared for beef. The breeds you are most likely to encounter are Hereford and Charolais, illustrated here. They are docile breeds – it is illegal for the farmer to keep breeds which are known to be temperamental (or *any* bull which has shown itself to be temperamental) in fields to which the public has access. Nevertheless, exercise extreme caution if you see a bull, particularly if you have a dog with you, which must, of course, be kept under strict control.

Those areas where you may see a bull in a field crossed by the Wolds Way are marked on the maps in this book.

The Humber

The wide, muddy Humber is followed for only five kilometres of the Wolds Way, but it is on this section – the very start – that you are likely to linger longest.

Sociologists claim that man is subconsciously attracted to the water-side, which is perhaps why so many people are to be found along this stretch, sitting in cars and staring out over the estuary. But there are certainly more tangible attractions, like the awesome new bridge and the constant stream of river traffic.

Although this is not exactly a place of outstanding scenic beauty, the view across to the south bank is pleasantly appealing, particularly opposite North Ferriby, where the Lincolnshire Wolds – a continuation of the same seam of chalk that rises northwards – descend gently to the river.

The Humber has played an important part in the formation of the Wolds landscape, its colonisation and the development of agriculture and industry throughout the entire region. It is, of course, not a river but the confluence of the Trent and the Yorkshire Ouse. Altogether one-fifth of England's land surface, some 25,000 square kilometres, is drained into the Humber. Its main course was formed when the chalk-beds rose unevenly through movement of the earth's crust over 70 million years ago. The ridge of chalk was cut by rivers in several places, notably the Humber.

Today the river can be divided into two distinct sections. The first, which is the original stretch, runs east for about 28 kilometres as far as Hessle and once emptied into Bridlington Bay over 50 kilometres farther north from its present exit to the North Sea. The second, which runs south-east for 30 kilometres, follows a channel that was excavated by meltwater through glacial deposits at a late stage in the Ice Age.

For centuries there has been a continual change in the appearance of the Humber. The tide has been eating away at the boulder clay of the Holderness coast, south of Flamborough, ever since the Ice Age created it 25,000 years ago. This silt or 'warp' has been carried up the estuary by the flood-tide and deposited at slackwater. Thus the town of Hedon to the east of Hull is 2.5 kilometres from the sea, although in medieval times it was not only by the water's edge but was also the most prosperous port on the Humber.

The north bank of the Humber's gain has been the Holderness coast's great loss. A score of villages have been slowly washed away since medieval times, while the narrow gravel spit of Spurn Head at the mouth of the estuary has been subjected to a cycle of destruction and re-creation. It has remained stable for a century because of artificial sea defences but these are crumbling fast and it is thought that the peninsula, which is managed as a nature reserve by the Yorkshire Naturalists' Trust, will soon enter the erosion and growth cycle again unless the defences are re-fortified.

Farther up the Humber there has been extensive land reclamation, notably the creation in 1827 of Reads Island off South Ferriby, which can be seen from the point where the Wolds Way begins the trek away from the shore. It is believed that accretion began around the wreck of a large sailing vessel which had foundered on a sandbank. Thirteen years later there were 30 hectares for grazing cattle and sheep and this grew to 199 hectares until a cycle of erosion began to stabilise the island's size.

Man first navigated the Humber between the tenth and eighth centuries BC. The evidence for this is a 14.5-metre 'dug-out' boat found in 1886 beside the River Ancholme at Brigg on South Humberside. Formed from one huge oak tree, hollowed out by fire and primitive hand-tools, it was the earliest prehistoric boat recorded in Britain. Later, it went on display in Hull's Albion Museum along with many relics from the Yorkshire Wolds. Alas, the museum received a direct hit during a blitz in 1943 and the boat and the bulk of the region's archaeological treasures disintegrated.

Finds of more advanced boats, made of planks sewn together with yew withies, were made at North Ferriby. These were from the Late Bronze Age (890-590 BC), and indicate that passage on the Humber was becoming increasingly regular.

As sea travel became more sophisticated and as men came from the Continent to explore, they found the Humber an open door that was irresistible. Around 300 BC warrior bands of invaders arrived from the Marne region of Northern France. These people, the Parisii who gave their name to the capital of France, brought with them skills as cultivators and herdsmen. They spread quickly over the Wolds and they have left their mark on the landscape in earthworks near Huggate and Millington and the chariot burial at Arras.

The Humber was at one time the frontier of the Roman conquest. In AD 70 it was forded and the first regular ferry on the river established between what is now Winteringham on the south bank, and Brough (then named *Petuaria*) just west of North Ferriby. The ferry became an essential link on the Roman road between Lincoln and York.

The North Ferriby boat – a reconstruction
(*By kind permission of the Kingston-upon-Hull City Museums*)

Next came the Saxons who sailed up the Humber in the sixth century. Two centuries later came Viking invaders in their longships, followed 100 years on by a large fleet of Danish settlers.

Perhaps the most famous sailors on the Humber did not come upstream but left its wide mouth far behind. They were the Pilgrim Fathers, who left Killingholme or Immingham Creek, on the south bank, in 1608 to sail for Holland before eventually crossing the Atlantic in 1620.

For six centuries highly characteristic sailing-vessels have plied the Humber. Just as the Thames barge, the Norfolk wherry and the Tyne brig were developed to suit local conditions, so the Humber keel and sloop, to name a couple, were produced.

The keel, flat-bottomed and with a square rig, is the most distinctive and is thought to be a direct descendant of the Viking longship. (They, of course, were quite a regular sight on the Humber for a couple of centuries.) Keels were used mainly on the rivers and canals and many of them were built by Richard Dunstons, the shipyard beside Hessle Haven right at the very start of the Wolds Way.

The sloop was similar but had too wide a beam for canals, restricting its use more to the Humber estuary and to the tidal stretches of the Trent and Ouse. An advantage of the wider beam was an increase in cargo capacity. The main difference between the two craft, however, was the rig. The keel had a mainsail and topsail, the latter used mostly on canals. The sloop had a fore-and-aft arrangement of mainsail and jib.

Both craft were active well into the present century. The most popular vessels on the Humber, however, were the ferries. They have only just ceased to operate.

There has been a cross-river service of sorts for centuries and sometimes it was a pretty rough crossing. Daniel Defoe, for example, records that he was 'near four hours tossed about' between Barton and Hull. He went back and wrote about a character named Robinson Crusoe, who also had a rather rough voyage and who had set out from the Port of Hull.

The first Hull-to-New Holland service began in the late 1820s, in a wooden paddler that had coaches waiting for it on the south bank for the onward journey to London.

The end of a very long line of coal-fired paddle steamers was the *Lincoln Castle,* which broke down in 1978 and was considered not worth repairing, with the opening of the Humber Bridge apparently just months away. In fact, the last ferry to operate the run, the diesel-powered *Farringford,* had to sail on for another three years before the bridge was ready. You will find the *Lincoln Castle,* ironically, beside the Humber Bridge, and leading a new life as restaurant and bar.

The bridging of the Humber was probably inevitable. Economically, it made little sense because, as many local critics have said, 'it joins nowt with nowt!' meaning that it is too far off the motorway thoroughfare of Britain to justify its cost of £91 million.

The idea for a fixed link between two sides of the river started life as a plan for a railway tunnel. In 1872 the Hull, South and West Junction Railway drew up proposals for a tunnel costing £960,000, supported by a petition of 10,000 signatures from the people of Hull. But the House of Lords rejected the scheme, mainly on engineering grounds.

Next came the idea of a railway bridge, encouraged by the impressive structure that had, in the 1880s, been put across the River Forth. The railway companies realised that they

Humber sloop and keel *c.* 1910

Artist's impression of the proposed 1931 Humber Bridge
(*By kind permission of the Hull Daily Mail*)

could not fund such a project themselves and no money was forthcoming from the government. It was not until the 1920s, when many large civil engineering schemes were initiated around the country, that the road became a serious proposal. Local authorities on both sides of the river appointed bridge consultants, who came up with a detailed design for a multi-span steel girder bridge. It looked faintly reminiscent of the Forth rail bridge. But a Bill setting up a Bridge Board was lost when Ramsay MacDonald's government collapsed in the 1931 economic crisis.

By the early 1960s the Forth had been bridged for traffic and the Severn was about to be bridged. The Humber Bridge was not far behind. It got the formal go-ahead in 1969 and work began in July 1972.

No chapter on the Humber is complete without a special mention of Hull. The city began as a small community founded by monks in the twelfth century and it was the deep-water channel's preference at that time for a more northerly slant down the Humber that led to Hull and neighbouring Hedon becoming ports. In the late sixteenth century, Hull was one of many ports to get into the expanding whaling industry to provide for the growing demand for whale oil, but it fell into decline during the reign of Charles II and the monopoly passed temporarily to the Dutch. The revival ended in the mid-nineteenth century when a government bounty for the industry was withdrawn.

But then came a find that was to change Hull's history. In 1843 a fishing smack from Brixham, in Devon, working out of Scarborough at the time, discovered the famous Silver Pits on the Dogger Bank, about 100 kilometres off the Humber. Huge catches of sole were made by every vessel that went to have a go and the best placed ports to exploit this vast new resource were at Hull and Grimsby. At the same time, the railway boom was reaching a peak and Hull was well connected for getting the fish, while still fresh, to the rest of England.

By 1863 Hull alone had 270 fishing vessels but as the industry grew the stocks were run down and the trawler owners, flush with more wealth than they knew what to do with, invested in bigger boats and new equipment. Ice was taken to sea to slow down the deterioration of fish and then steam trawlers made it possible for skippers to explore the waters of the Northern hemisphere.

But it was all at considerable cost. The people of Hull have lived with sudden bereavement on a mass scale for over a century. One hundred years ago, one per cent of the total male workforce was lost at sea every year. On one day alone in 1883, a fleet was devastated in a North Sea gale and an estimated 360 men and boys from Hull were drowned. The last great trawler disaster was in February 1974, when all 36 men on the highly sophisticated 'unsinkable' *Gaul* were lost off northern Norway, the vessel apparently having been hit by a series of freak waves.

The industry is now dying: Britain has been increasingly turned out of her traditional fishing grounds as countries like Iceland and Norway have insisted on keeping their diminishing fish stocks to themselves, and a whole way of life for Humberside folk is vanishing. It was the hardest of lives: I well remember being horrified at conditions when I spent some time on a trawler off Iceland, reporting the 1975-6 Cod War. The lasting impression is one of the freezing conditions on the decks, as men worked shifts day and night, and of the overpowering smell of cooking, tobacco and putrefying cod livers below decks.

The Wolds landscape

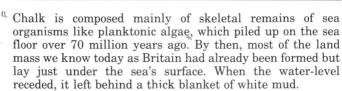

Chalk is composed mainly of skeletal remains of sea organisms like planktonic algae, which piled up on the sea floor over 70 million years ago. By then, most of the land mass we know today as Britain had already been formed but lay just under the sea's surface. When the water-level receded, it left behind a thick blanket of white mud.

These chalk-beds initially covered a very wide area and were thrust even higher by movement in the earth's crust. But volcanic eruptions on the north-west side, and the opening up of the Atlantic Ocean, eroded much of the infant chalk landscape.

There remained a belt extending from the Channel through Devon and Dorset and Kent, Sussex and Surrey, northwards to form the Marlborough and Berkshire Downs and then dipping under the Wash to reappear as the Wolds. Many changes in the belt's appearance followed, notably the advent of new rivers draining across Britain from west to east. The mightiest of these was the Humber estuary, which cut through the final northward thrust of chalk – thus creating separate Lincolnshire and Yorkshire Wolds.

Later, the Ice Age produced further changes. The rounded slopes were broken by valleys through which much water ran when the ice thawed. Chalk is easily dissolved and most of the waterways have either dried up or gone underground, leaving 'dry valleys'.

Over millions of years, nature has carved some of the easiest land to cultivate, making it hardly surprising that England's chalk downlands hosted the earliest farmers in this country.

The Yorkshire Wolds were quickly colonised when man began to work the land over 5,000 years ago and since then hardly a square metre of the rolling hills and their intimate valleys has not been used for either primitive or modern agriculture. A good living has been obtained by tilling the light soils and grazing stock on the sweet chalk pastures.

Today, the face of the Wolds is one of grassed-over scars and pock-marks left by earlier peoples and the area is,

arvesting
ear
illington

15

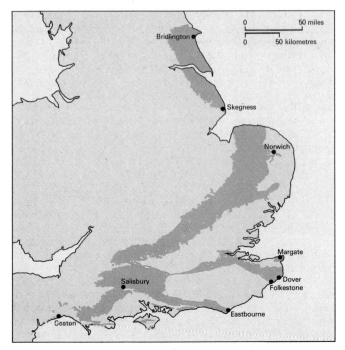

The extent of the chalk in England

consequently, one vast classroom for the archaeologist. Among the finds are barrows and earthworks, standing stones and boats, pottery and flint implements: they tell a story of a landscape that was very busy several thousand years ago.

All the signs are that prehistoric man preferred the Wolds to the lowlands. There are varying theories to account for this. The vegetation on the chalk hills was certainly easy to clear and the light soil was amenable to cultivation without sophisticated methods and implements. Also, early man felt safer on high ground. And the alternatives were not very attractive: all around the Wolds were carrs (flat lands liable to seasonal flooding).

Yet the very earliest settlers undoubtedly chose the low-lying areas of East Yorkshire. These were mesolithic peoples, between 10,000 to 4000 BC. They arrived when the ice-sheet retreated and chose the edges of wide marshes, where they could live on fish, wildfowl, nuts and shellfish. At Starr Carr, in the once marshy Vale of Pickering to the north-west of the Wolds, arrow and harpoon heads made of bone have been found, whereas no such obvious traces of these people have turned up in the chalk hills.

It was in neolithic times, from 3250 to around 1700 BC, when man stopped being a predator and began producing his own food, that the colonisation of the Wolds really began.

This revolution in life style, with stored grain providing a continuous food supply – very different from the hand-to-mouth existence of the hunter – brought a large increase in population on the Continent and in the Mediterranean region. And so many people set off in search of new land.

The first neolithic people to make an impact on the Wolds can be traced not by their settlements but by their burial sites. Their long barrow burial chambers are the most noted archaeological treasures on the hills. The barrow at Duggleby Howe, near Wharram le Street, was probably built before 2500 BC. It is six metres high and contains remains of 53 cremations, antler tools and a flint knife. A study of the Ordnance Survey maps shows that the entire area of the Wolds is covered with field monuments called tumuli.

By the time of the Bronze Age, most of the Wolds had been cleared for cultivation and a picture emerges of a patchwork of small, irregular strips of ploughed hillside. This was what the Beaker Folk, the first metal-using invaders of Britain (from 1900 BC onwards) found when they arrived.

The best-known early invaders of the Wolds were the La Tène people from northern France, who arrived in the early Iron Age from around 300 BC onwards. They were warlike bands under powerful chiefs. The tribe which invaded Yorkshire were the Parisii whose major preoccupation appears to have been constructing great lengths of earthworks. Some of the best examples are around Huggate and Millington, close to the Wolds Way.

These warriors lived in great fear of their chieftains. When they died, the latter were buried in square barrows, on lower Wolds slopes. Finds of these Parisii barrows have been made at Arras, close to the Wolds Way (see page 46).

The next wave of people to arrive on the Wolds were the

Sword found at North Grimston and associated with the Parisii culture
(*By kind permission of the Kingston-upon-Hull City Museums*)

Romans in around AD 71. The roads, forts and signal stations of Roman occupation very quickly appeared, spreading from the encampment at York, which was then called *Eboracum*. The Parisii were assimilated into the Roman system as farmers and turned to Roman ways of farming, including a preference for large corn-growing areas instead of predominantly livestock farms.

When the Angles began to arrive in force around AD 450, it was to watch for them that the Romans built a signal station on Carr Naze, on the Wolds Way above Filey Brigg. It was natural that they should want to stay: the land was prosperous and the Roman villas and roads made life and communications a lot easier than they were used to. The Angles, and later the Danes, stayed for several centuries, founding many new village settlements. The names still remain today: Brantingham, Goodmanham and Everingham were early Saxon settlements; Welton and Millington came later; villages with names ending with 'by' and 'thorpe' were founded by Danish settlers.

Chalk is a permeable rock and water is quickly absorbed. To begin with, most settlements were on the lower slopes of the Wolds, where springs provided water but later the Anglo-Saxons realised that water could be trapped in saucers of clay. These were the beginnings of the village ponds at places like Huggate and Fridaythorpe. There are few streams on chalkland and the most interesting water course is the Gypsey Race, running through the Wolds (underground for most of the time) from Duggleby to Bridlington. These erratic streams or 'races' are known elsewhere as 'bournes'.

Throughout the Anglo-Saxon period the Wolds landscape continued to be transformed by new agricultural methods. Before 1066, much of the land was divided up and it is thought that the boundaries which were made at this time form the basis of the parishes which exist today. The method of agriculture was basically the open-field system, which was in use until the time of the agricultural revolution around the end of the eighteenth century.

The Norman Conquest produced a major setback for some areas of the Wolds: the 'harrying of the North' drove many people away from their settlements and much land was wasted. In early medieval times, the arable fields were restored, much scrub was cleared and the new Norman lords went all out to produce large amounts of corn for a rapidly expanding population. But in the summer of 1349, the Black Death brought much suffering and de-population to Yorkshire. Many buildings and farms were abandoned. Then in the late fourteenth and fifteenth centuries, there was a great shift in the emphasis of Wolds farming, from crop-production to sheep-rearing, and many villages – Wharram Percy being the best known – were abandoned as the Wolds became vast sheep-walks.

That picture remained virtually unaltered until the eighteenth century when the Wolds landscape we know today began to take shape. The person responsible for the transformation was undoubtedly Sir Christopher Sykes of Sledmere. With his wife's vast fortune, he enclosed many of the sheep-walks and ploughed up the springy pastures to find a light, thin soil that was ideal for cereal-growing. Barley-growing was his first major innovation but he also planted thousands of hectares of larch trees as copses. Within 30 years his enterprise was being copied throughout the Wolds, turning the land into what was described at the time as 'one of the most productive and best cultivated districts in the County of York'.

The enclosure of pasture-land continued well into this century, the most controversial being that of Millington Pasture in the 1960s. Few sheep-walks remain. Virtually the only traditional chalk pastures remaining in the Wolds are the steep-sided banks of the dry valleys and it is now uncertain whether even these beautiful banks, with their highly individual chalkland flora, will survive. Already, the sloping pastures on the downland of southern England are disappearing because of agricultural improvement.

Other changes have taken place in the Wolds landscape as a result of the demands of modern agriculture. Many plantations have been cut down and not replaced; many hedges have been grubbed out to create huge fields of corn and barley; and as farms have become bigger, so buildings that were there from the seventeenth and eighteenth centuries have disappeared.

Today, visitors will notice a richness and intensity of farming in the Wolds, accounted for by the quality of the soil, which is good at the northern end and even better towards the south and the Humber shore. It is a medium to heavy loam, lightened and drained by the presence of stones, which are mainly chalk. Characteristic of the Wolds are the dry dales, the slopes of which have soil that is not so good, having been eroded down into the dale bottoms where the soil is deep.

The farm structure reflects at least two stages in the development of the landscape: firstly, the growth of the medieval villages and the smallholdings that surrounded them; secondly, the creation, out on the Wolds themselves, of large farms during the time of land enclosure between 1750 and 1850. This pattern of land ownership and farm size still exists.

Farming in the Wolds is typical of low-rainfall east-coast areas. Ninety-five per cent of the land is under arable cultivation, of which 60-65 per cent is taken up by cereal crops, winter wheat, spring and winter barley. The remainder is mostly under grass for grazing, oil-seed rape or vining peas. The acreage of oil-seed rape increased dramatically in the late 1970s and early 1980s: at least 8,000 hectares were grown in Humberside in 1980 and the area is probably the

Straw bales and a tractor-drawn baler

second most important for this crop in the country. It is a crop of benefit to all: as well as supplying animal feed it also contributes to a whole range of processed foods, notably cooking oils and margarine. The distinctive yellow flower provides exceptionally colourful patches on the Wolds landscape in spring.

The most numerous livestock found on the Wolds is still sheep: there are an estimated 200,000 ewes and lambs in these chalk hills. No one breed is characteristic of the area as it is, for example, in the Yorkshire Dales. There is a variety of crosses. Sheep come into their own in the farming of the dry dales because the dale sides are often too steep and the soils too poor for cultivation.

Both dairy and beef cattle are reared on the Wolds. Again there are no regional breeds and the most commonly seen are black and white Friesian and Holstein, while some farmers are experimenting with the more recently introduced breeds like Charolais and Limousin.

If you ask a farmer what he thinks of the Wolds, he may detain you for over an hour, talking about the quality of the soil, how the land dries out quickly and how there are good drying winds always blowing over the gentle hills.

The next significant use of the Wolds, of course, is for leisure. The Wolds Way's official designation is an early sign that this is happening and the area's narrow lanes are increasingly being explored by touring cyclists and, despite rising petrol prices, by motorists who have tired of the crowds in the Yorkshire Dales and the North York Moors.

The coast

Chalk builds the 'white walls of Old England'. Our most distinctive coastal scenery consists of dazzling precipices undermined by the restless tide, which has created shining, green-capped stacks.

Chalk forms only a small part of the British coastline, however, and is usually associated with the English Channel – thanks to *The White Cliffs of Dover*. But the most interesting stretch of chalk coast is arguably the 16 kilometres round Flamborough Head into Filey Bay, the northernmost limit of British chalk.

These cliffs resemble, in some ways, the white walls of the Channel as they looked until earlier this century. There have been few developments on the cliff-tops and the tiny fishing communities at North and South Landing are much as they were 50 years ago and will remain so, protected, as they are, by their 'Heritage Coast' definition. But the biggest difference is that the Yorkshire chalk still supports tens of thousands of nesting seabirds, while the cliffs in the Channel – the world's busiest shipping lane – have gradually lost most of their birds as pollution has become commonplace.

There is little sign of the scarred precipices of Flamborough and Bempton losing their vast populations. Even when the eggs were harvested annually and their whites used as softeners in the Leeds tanneries – as many as 130,000 eggs a year until the practice was halted by the Protection of Birds Act 1954 – the birds thrived.

Little seems to change on the Yorkshire coast. Little, that is, except the coast itself. South of Flamborough the Holderness coast suffers the worst erosion in Europe as the soft boulder clay that was a gift of the Ice Age is swept away by the North Sea. The same process has been going on to a much lesser extent on the other side of the chalk, at Filey Bay. The result has been the creation of a superb bathing bay, a natural shelter for boats and the best stretch of sand on the Yorkshire coast. There are nine kilometres of fine sand which, at low tide, have been used as a runway for aeroplanes. In 1910 the Blackburn Aeroplane Company of Leeds arrived in Filey and tested a new monoplane on the sand for almost a year, until the first successful flight was made in March 1911.

Now the beach is a popular meeting place for wind-surfers

Kittiwake

Fulmar

Gannet

Guillemot

Razorbill

Rock doves

Puffins

Meadow
pipit

Scentless mayweed

Yarrow

and the bay is a colourful scene of racing-dinghies most summer weekends.

Erosion of the bay has undoubtedly been slowed by the protective arm of Filey Brigg, a massive slab of lower calcareous gritstone. It is thought that the name derives from the Scandinavian *bryggja,* meaning jetty or landing place.

Many people have met their deaths out on the Brigg: anglers swept away by ferocious waves, and fishermen whose small flat-bottomed boats known as cobles have come to grief on the jagged rocks. The promontory has been responsible for many wrecks and one of the best remembered locally was in 1928 when a Norwegian vessel foundered. The crew landed safely, while her cargo of herring was later washed ashore, and Filey people, it is said, were never so well fed.

The seas along the entire coastline hide many wrecks. Between 1914 and 1918 alone there were 17 recorded sinkings in Filey Bay. One fishing coble, the *Edith Cavell,* was torpedoed by a German U-boat and her crew taken aboard, only to be released at the Farne Islands. It is said that everyone in the town went to meet them on their return at Filey Station. Less certain are the tales by Filey and Flamborough fishermen of how German U-boats in the First World War surfaced off Flamborough and bought fish from the men they surprised in cobles.

At the end of last century, a Grimsby trawler foundered on rocks below Speeton cliffs, and the egg collectors – or 'climmers' as they were known – went down on their ropes to save the crew. As a result, the climmers, who were coming under pressure even then to stop their annual harvest, legitimised their activities by becoming coastguard auxiliaries, ready for future shipwrecks at the foot of the cliffs.

The most famous wreck off the coast is that of *Le Bonhomme Richard.* This was the ship of the American pirate John Paul Jones. In September 1779, Jones sailed down the east coast of Britain and learned that a convoy of merchant ships, escorted by two British men-of-war – HMS *Serapis* and *The Countess of Scarborough* – were in Bridlington Bay. Knowing that he could out-gun the British, Jones waited off Filey until his prey left on the tide that night. As the British vessels sailed round Flamborough Head, the pirate opened fire and the commander of the convoy eventually surrendered. But Jones's vessel went down shortly afterwards as a result of a direct hit. The battle was watched in the moonlight by the people of Flamborough and Filey, standing on the cliffs.

A commemorative plaque at Flamborough acknowledges John Paul Jones as the father of the US Navy and there has been recent activity by divers searching for his vessel off the point.

Like so many resorts, Filey developed in the eighteenth century as a spa town. The spring was out on the cliffs above the Brigg and although nothing of it remains today, it started

North cliffs, Filey

a holiday trade that grew throughout the Victorian age. The gentry of the West Riding were attracted to the spa town and to cater for them The Crescent, a late Georgian-style parade of houses overlooking the bay, was built around 1840. It could almost be a part of Brighton and some of the buildings have ornate features like Regency iron balconies.

The heart of the town was in the Church Street and Queen Street area and it is here that some of the most interesting buildings are found. Foords Hotel has Greek Doric columns at the doorway and, closer to the sea, there is the former T'Awd Ship Inn, once the centre of smuggling activities in Filey. Also in Queen Street is a folk museum in two cottages.

Filey's busiest area, however, is down at the Coble Landing. Here the highly distinctive fishing boats are kept. There is no natural harbour in the bay, so the boats have to be towed out to the water's edge and launched by tractor. Before tractors were in use, a team of two or three horses did the work.

The coble may have been developed as an open seaboat based on the Viking longship. The unique high bow and deep forefoot are essential for beach launching, and the flat stern allows beaching to take place even in rough weather. Generally, Filey cobles are lighter than those used elsewhere on the Yorkshire coast because of the difficult landing conditions.

In spring and summer, the drift-nets you see in Filey Bay catch salmon and trout. The season ends about the same time as the tourist season, and through the winter, a local fisherman tells me the men work at 'owt tha' maks a livin', which is mainly crabs, codlings and lobsters.

River to coast: a varied wildlife

Like the beauty of the Yorkshire Wolds, the area's wildlife treasures are not lavishly displayed but have to be sought out at specific points.

Along most of the footpath there is little variety since intensive farming leaves few areas of thick cover in which many different species can survive together. Hundreds of kilometres of hedgerows – many of them put down in the eighteenth century and rich in wild plants and animals – have been grubbed up since the Second World War. But the people who fashioned the Wolds Way have made the best of what the area has.

Thus the footpath links together a whole variety of habitats, from muddy shores and thickly wooded dells to high cereal-growing fields, deep valleys with steep grassy banks and, finally, rocky shores and vertical sea-cliffs.

So far as birdlife is concerned, some of the biggest concentrations are to be seen at either end of the Wolds Way. Muddy estuaries never fail to attract large numbers of birds at the spring and autumn migration times and since the Humber is one of the muddiest, it is teeming with birds.

The commonest species to be seen from the five kilometres of Wolds Way along the shore are dunlins and redshanks. They appear in vast numbers farther east on the great flats at Spurn Bight, but between Hessle and North Ferriby, particularly at low water, they are regularly seen probing the mud for sand-insects and sand-worms and wading in the shallow water at the edge in search of crustaceans.

It is inconceivable that you should pass this section without seeing mallard, wigeon or shelduck. The latter is one of the most beautiful ducks to be seen in Britain, with its handsome red bill, green head and mostly white body dressed with a chestnut mantle.

In spring and early summer you will most likely have the company of at least one neurotic lapwing, incessantly calling 'peewit' as it ushers you along the shore past its nest in an adjacent field. Look up and you will probably see a hovering kestrel, which loves grassy embankments like those carrying

Turnstone

Pink-footed
goose

Dunlin (in
Shelduck
Dunlin

the main Hull-to-Selby railway line along the Humber. These embankments are the habitat of its favourite food – mice and voles.

Throughout the autumn and early winter the Humber just west of North Ferriby is invaded by some 10,000 pink-footed geese – one-fifth of the number that comes to Britain each winter from east Greenland and central Iceland. They roost on Whitton Sand, near the outfall of the River Trent, and can be seen during the day feeding on the surrounding country-side. Their roost is now a wardened wildfowl refuge.

Blacktoft Sand, farther up the Humber, was one of the last British breeding places of the avocet before it became extinct on this side of the North Sea in 1837. (It returned to the Suffolk coast a century later.)

The birdlife of the Wolds is rather predictable. For almost every step along the footpath there will be the compan-ionship of skylarks. Not far away will be a few yellowham-mers, uttering loudly their distinctive call that sounds like 'a-little-bit-of-bread-and-no-cheese', and occasionally you will see its slightly plumper relative, the corn bunting. You will put up flocks of wood-pigeon and partridges from the

Redshank   Knot

fields and in the hedges, disturb wrens, chaffinches and – in spring and summer – willow warblers and whitethroats. You will remember woods like East Dale chiefly for their beautiful little parties of long-tailed tits and for the pheasants that startled you.

The Yorkshire Wolds are classic chalklands with their highly distinctive flora. There are harebells, bee-orchids, carline thistles and seemingly thousands of cowslips. Along the tops of the steep sides to the dry valleys are hawthorn scrub and gorse with its fragrant yellow flowers. The banks are full of meadow oat grass and sheep's fescue, wild thyme and wild basil. In summer the delicate white flowers found along most of the way are shepherd's purse, and the path is heavily overgrown with the familiar cow parsley and red clover.

The flora is a reflection of what is underneath. It is capable of surviving on well-drained slopes and in thin calcium-rich soils of chalk downland, as well as putting up with the constant cropping of rabbits and sheep, and cultivation by man.

Most of what you see in the high Wolds is in the vicinity of hedgerows. These are normally hawthorn and contain a great number of ash, which is the tree of chalkland, a lot of beech and sycamore, and some crab-apple. In the hedgebanks a large variety of shrubs and flowers such as bluebells, buttercups and red campion compete for the available light. On the northern stretches of the Wolds Way, also look out for scarlet pimpernel.

Virtually the last area of old Wolds grassland was at Millington Pasture, seen across a dale from the Wolds Way just south-west of Huggate. Much of this has disappeared as a result of enclosures in the 1960s but there are still some parts – mainly on the steep banks – where the traditional flora can be seen. It is much less varied than that of the chalk of southern England and botanists have found this valuable in making comparative studies with other parts of the country. Millington Pasture is recognised as a site of special scientific interest.

Some of the most rewarding times along the Wolds Way come when you sit down, perhaps at a stile in a hedgerow, to take a rest. If you are silent, there is a chance that you will find a weasel that has been stalking along the side of the hedge in search of mice and voles. If you are very lucky at the northern end of the footpath, you might even find a sparrowhawk dashing along the hedge trying to take a small bird by surprise.

Walking along the hedgerows in spring and summer, you are constantly attracted by some movement. It might be a roosting tawny owl that you have disturbed, or some of the many rabbits that now live freely in the Wolds (they were once farmed in huge warrens). You will continually find yourself watching a fluttering butterfly. They are common features of chalk country and the Yorkshire Wolds host some of the most beautiful. The common blue and the orange-tip were the two most often seen on my travels along the footpath, but I believe from naturalists in the area that ringlets, red admirals, large, small and green-veined whites, small tortoiseshells and brown arguses can also be seen. The most interesting places for plants and butterflies are the old chalk pits, particularly those owned or leased as reserves by the Yorkshire Naturalists' Trust. These include Fordon Chalk Bank, south of Camp Dale; Kipling Cotes Chalk Pit and related disused railway line; Rifle Butts Quarry, near Goodmanham; and Wharram Quarry, near Wharram le Street. Access to some of these is by arrangement (see address on page 107).

Many farmers can tell you of foxes in the Wolds and there are also stories of where badgers can be found.

On the coast the main attraction is undoubtedly the huge concentration of seabirds. The northern extremity of British chalk is the vertical white wall that plunges into the North Sea for 16 kilometres from the south side of Filey Bay round the great promontory of Flamborough Head, and it is here

Orange tip

Common blue

Curlew

Cowslip

Bee orchid

Forget-me-not

Shepherd's purse

Buttercup

that tens of thousands of birds nest precariously every year.

Bempton Cliffs, the gleaming precipice 120 metres high seen across the bay from Filey Brigg, are protected as a reserve by the Royal Society for the Protection of Birds. Their most interesting feature in recent years has been the establishment of the only nesting colony of gannets on mainland Britain. This started in the 1950s with less than 10 pairs and by 1970 it had grown to just under 30. The expansion took place throughout the next decade until a count in 1980 showed 280 nesting pairs present. The huge white bird can be seen diving off Filey Brigg throughout the summer.

Along the entire coast are great numbers of kittiwakes, 65,000 at Bempton alone and another 16,000 at Flamborough. Guillemots and razorbills are numerous and there must be up to 2,500 puffins. All of these species are seen on the cliffs to the north of Filey Brigg, right at the very end of the Wolds Way. At a couple of viewpoints overlooking Brewster Hole, a small rocky bay just before the Cleveland Way takes over for the rest of the Yorkshire coast, it is possible to see several pairs of cormorants nesting below on the wider ledges.

Filey Brigg is one of the best points on the entire east coast of Britain for watching migratory birds. And there is good reason to choose the Brigg: some of the surprise feathered visitors to this coast have included long-tailed skuas from the far north, little shearwaters from the eastern mid-Atlantic, and sooty shearwaters from the south Atlantic.

Not every bird is a rarity: in autumn fieldfares and redwings can be seen in large flocks coming down on the cliffs above the Brigg, their first landfall since flying across the North Sea from nesting grounds in Scandinavia. And most of the time turnstones, purple sandpipers and knots can be seen picking through the seaweed out on the reef.

The Wolds Way is routed along the cliff-tops because the tides are notoriously dangerous and the use of the shore path from Filey to the Brigg, therefore, is best left to people who know the state of the tide and the area. But at low tide (check the board at Coble Landing) the shore is definitely the best place to be. Up in the cliffs there are colonies of sand-martins. Below, the rocky pools are fun to explore.

oastline
ear Filey

Hessle to South Cave

20 kilometres

The starting point on the Wolds Way is more in view of the Lincolnshire Wolds than their Yorkshire continuation. You have several kilometres of muddy riverbank to walk before earning a glimpse of the southern extremity of chalk that you will follow to the sea.

ımber
ıdge

There is nothing significant about the footpath's beginning at the Ferry Boat Inn, beside Hessle Haven. It is chosen because of the nearby availability of car-parking space. Both buses and trains to Hessle – a small leafy town of 14,000 which has retained its individuality despite being virtually absorbed by Hull – are frequent from Hull city centre every day except Sunday.

A foot-bridge leads south from Hessle station and the inn is reached by a left-hand turn on Livingstone Road. Bus travellers should find the southern road out of Hessle Square and keep walking towards the river.

By the Haven is the last remaining large shipyard on the Humber. Here, many of the Humber's distinctive flat-bottomed keel-boats were built for use right up to the early part of this century.

Walk down to the river from the inn, turn right and follow the well-defined path along the shore towards a scene totally dominated by one of Britain's finest man-made creations – the Humber Bridge. In dry weather, crowds of gapers can be seen at a huge viewing area and walkers will feel inclined to join them in tilting their heads backwards to stare at the gigantic steel structure sweeping across the river.

Opened by the Queen on 17 July 1981, it is the longest single-span suspension bridge in the world. The distance between the two anchorages is 2,220 metres, 112 metres longer than its nearest rival, the Verrazano Narrows Bridge across the entrance to New York Harbour, which linked Brooklyn with Staten Island in 1964. The Humber Bridge took more than eight years to build, cost £91 million and was the subject of a local campaign for a century.

√elton

Held in a concrete pen by the bridge is the *Lincoln Castle,*

Lincoln Castle before her retirement

one of a series of three ferries which carried cars and passengers between Hull and New Holland for over 40 years. She was the last of a long line of coal-fired paddlers on the Humber, first appearing in 1940 and finally invalided out of service in March 1978, with boiler failure. It would have taken £10,000 to put her back in action and with the bridge's opening then seeming so imminent the work was considered a bad investment. Her fate was the same as that of many old steamers in Britain in the last 30 years – serving the lucrative bar-and-restaurant trade for people who like to enjoy an evening out in unusual surroundings.

The path leads under the bridge immediately beside the huge concrete legs of the 155-metre-high north-bank tower. The roadway carrying traffic backwards and forwards between Hessle and Barton-on-Humber is suspended some 30 metres above the water at high tide, leaving ample clearance for river traffic, which consists mainly of barges and coasters for the Ouse and Trent ports. Walking westwards along the shore, you will see the river craft closely following the north bank. Before the pier was constructed to take the south-bank tower of the bridge, the navigable channel was on the southern side, but Humber pilots think the buttress of the bridge diverted the water to the north side. An unexpected bonus was that the journey between Hull and Goole was cut by two kilometres and provided a saving in sailing time of six or seven minutes.

One-fifth of England's rivers provide the brown waters flowing down the Humber. On calm, sunny days the river hardly appears to move at all, but in stormy weather the muddy waters can be as rough as at any coast. Beachcombing along the shore is unrewarding; but bird-watching can be quite productive. Shelduck are present at most times of year, along with redshanks, dunlins and herons.

Running with the path for most of the way is the main railway line from Hull. It is from here that the Hull poet Philip Larkin observed in his famous poem *The Whitsun Weddings* that across the river is 'where sky and Lincolnshire and water meet'. The wide view across to the south bank is, indeed, interesting on a day of grey skies when the opposite shore and clouds appear to merge. Rising next to Barton-on-Humber is the northern shoulder of the Lincolnshire Wolds.

In order to stop the erosion of the shore there are quite a few sections of made-up defence rocks called gabions held in place by a sturdy steel mesh. Above that, the main wall is the embankment carrying the railway line. In spring and summer it hosts a sizeable colony of voles and shrews, attracting the almost continuous interest of hovering kestrels. Ahead, the view is dominated by the smoking chimney of Capper Pass Cement Works, behind North Ferriby. There is a similar scene across the river at South Ferriby. The stacks of cement works trailing smoke across the area are a common sight at the foot of chalk scarps because locally quarried chalk is used for the making of cement.

The path runs for a time with a fence on the right, at the end of which it joins the shingle beach (take care at high tide). Past the bottom houses of North Ferriby, aim for the start of the aptly named Long Plantation. Europe's oldest known plank-built boats were excavated on the shore in 1946. They were carefully constructed of planks sewn together with yew withies and were found in 1938 and 1940. Carbon dating put them in the late Bronze Age, suggesting that navigation of the Humber was regular even as early as 890-590 BC. A model can be seen in Hull's Transport and Archaeology Museum.

Once at the wood, the Wolds Way continues through the second entrance into the trees. The path is very muddy in places as it passes through the wood, mainly of sycamore, which shelters North Ferriby from the prevailing westerly wind and also screens the ugly chimney of Capper Pass.

The path emerges on the A63 road, the main road from Hull to the motorway network. It continues almost opposite on the other side of the road, but, for safety's sake, it might be better to cross this very busy dual carriageway by turning left and using the foot-bridge. A signpost points north by a stile on the edge of Terrace Plantation and the roar of traffic is soon lost as the path ascends, very gradually, the first toe of the Wolds. In summer the air is heavy with honeysuckle.

The path reaches a junction and the Wolds Way continues straight across into the trees, where after a short while a stile leads into a scout camp. Carry on through, descending to a road where you are confronted with the buildings used by Melton Bottom Quarry, almost one kilometre across and the largest chalk quarry in the Wolds. Almost directly opposite, take the road past the quarry workings and on the left at

Bow Plantation. Away to the left are fine views of the Humber. As the wood takes a left turn a kilometre farther on, the Wolds Way cuts through the wood to the right to a junction of lanes by a gate. Turn left on the lane which becomes Chapel Hill, into the village of Welton, one of the most pleasant of Hull's commuter villages.

St. Helen's Church, Welton, is in a beautiful setting of picturesque cottages and sparkling stream. It was restored by Sir Giles Gilbert Scott in 1863 and offends purist students of architecture as 'unemotional'. The less critical will find little to offend the eye in the centre of Welton. The Green Dragon in Cowgate is the inn where the famous highwayman Dick Turpin is alleged to have been arrested. Inside is a facsimile of the record of his arrest in 1739 for stealing horses across the river in Lincolnshire. The story goes that he drove them across the then quite shallow Humber to sell them in Yorkshire and got drunk one night at the inn, shot a gamecock, and was arrested. Thus it was discovered that he was not John Palmer, as he claimed, but Dick Turpin, the terror of coaching people across Hampstead Heath. He subsequently went to the gallows at York.

In spring, the stream is a magnet for small boys with tadpole nets, and flows into a pond populated with fat, well-fed mallards and shaded with willows.

The Wolds Way forks immediately to the right at the foot of Chapel Hill, up Dale Road, and leads past a pleasant modern development of houses; the attractive eighteenth-century Welton Lodge; and Welton Mill (which ceased operations only in the 1960s).

Through the garden of Dale Cottage, a stile leads to Welton Dale, our first experience of a typical Wolds dry valley and surely one of the prettiest. The plantation on the left – mainly conifers, ash and beech – was established in the Victorian era as part of the 'spirit of improvement' that became fashionable with more caring landowners. The whole dale echoes with bird-song. At the dalehead, go over the stile, continue into Welton Wold Plantation and enter a large clearing. Up in the trees to the left is a mausoleum built in 1818 by the Raikes family, the last owners of Welton House, but it is not accessible by a public path.

The Wolds Way turns down into a dip on the right through the wood to a stile on to a farm road. Across the road is another stile and the now familiar Wolds Way sign, which leads into a field, where you turn right, parallel with the road, towards a plantation and then turn northwards with the plantation on your left. For the first time, this is the kind of country that will become familiar along the Way to Filey: everything is cultivated, the scene a huge patchwork of different shades of green, yellow and brown.

Wauldby Manor Farm ahead was once the site of a fair-sized hamlet which gradually shrank because many of the pre-enclosure houses and farm buildings were poorly

Wauldby Manor Farm

constructed. Only the farm and the tiny church remain. By the pond, turn left and then sharp right, keeping to the right of the high hawthorn hedge and eventually joining a good track. This curves down to a gate, where a left turn leads on to a good lane sheltered by tall hawthorn hedges with lots of pink campion in the banks in summer. Go straight up the road ahead until it bends left, then carry on up the green lane. Looking back, you can see a pretty good section of the ground already covered by the Wolds Way, as well as clear views of South Humberside and South Yorkshire. Once the track becomes a metalled road, look for the end of the plantation on the right; cross into the field and head towards the two large trees on the far side in the dip and then towards a gate next to the cottage.

Down the road to the left is the village of Brantingham. Those who go exploring will be most struck by the memorial to the dead of the First World War. The stone is made from bits and pieces taken from the Hull Town Hall when, in 1914, it was reconstructed as the Guildhall. The memorial has been described as 'lovably awful'.

Our path turns right on to the road past the church which, if not the most attractive in the district, is greatly improved by its backdrop of conifer-mantled hills. This is one of several of the architect G. E. Street's restorations for the second Sir Tatton Sykes – there are several more along the Way.

Brantingham Dale, which the route turns up, is the most popular valley outside Hull for weekend motorists. Look for a gate and stile on the left leading into a charming little dale full of bird-song and young sycamore, but marred by the

Brantingham Church

sight of huge electricity pylons. At the top there is a stile to cross before joining a track sloping downhill to a path, which slants to the right of the farm towards a gate. On the other side, the path leads down into a dip and then strikes up the other side to the top corner of Woodale Plantation. Continue north-west, passing Mount Airy Farm and turning sharp left at the end of the farmyard and then follow the path round down the hill to meet a metalled road. To the left is the village of South Cave, where there is accommodation and refreshment. The Wolds Way continues across the field ahead, over a stile in the hedge a short distance down the road.

South Cave to Goodmanham

18 kilometres

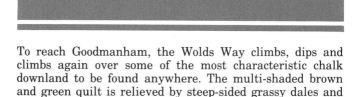

To reach Goodmanham, the Wolds Way climbs, dips and climbs again over some of the most characteristic chalk downland to be found anywhere. The multi-shaded brown and green quilt is relieved by steep-sided grassy dales and thickly wooded dells. On the airy tops the views to the west are extensive and – always – there is the singing of skylarks.

South Cave is mainly another dormitory village for Hull, its population of around 3,000 having trebled since the Second World War. But it is a very ancient settlement, lying on the old Roman road from Lincoln to York. In 1291 and 1313 it was granted a Royal Charter for a market. The eighteenth-century market-hall still stands in the centre.

For those not visiting the village, the route continues across the road from the track leading to Mount Airy Farm. Rejoin the footpath from South Cave by walking up the road, which leads to the tiny hamlet of Riplingham and on to Beverley. The footpath can also be reached by Little Wold Lane, seen on the left on the road out of South Cave. Once over the stile, ascend the hill ahead gradually with the hedge first on the left and then on the right, turning to the right with Little Wold Plantation. A well-placed seat by the side of the wood is a good point from which to admire a wide view of the Humber. On the horizon is the steelworks at Scunthorpe.

The wood is mainly beech and has a lush pile of ground-ivy. The track is framed by mature deciduous trees and there are thick banks of nettles and cow parsley. Emerging on a track (actually an unmaintained county road), turn right down a slope with high hedges on either side, until you reach the secluded Comber Dale on the left. Go over a stile and descend the slope where, in spring, the many hawthorn trees are dusted white with blossom. Ahead in the trees are Weedley Springs, the source of the stream running into North Cave. It is the best example of a natural spring encountered on the Wolds Way. At the bottom, curve around to the right to Weedley Dale, down and through a gate on to the old railway.

This route once carried the most ambitious railway track ever laid in East Yorkshire, the Hull-to-Barnsley line, which opened on 20 July 1885. The project was conceived to 'break the neck of the monopolies', specifically that of the North-East Railway Company. A new company was formed, the Alexandra Dock was built in Hull to give the port the best coal-handling facilities on the east coast and the direct rail link with the coalfield of the West Riding was constructed. At first the massive project, requiring a labour force of 4,900 men, appeared to be a great success, with coal shipments almost quadrupling within 15 years of the line's opening. But the North-East Railway simply lowered its charges to compete and the new company was soon in financial difficulties. The inevitable merger came in 1921, but traffic never lived up to expectations and the line closed in April 1959. Its construction had involved considerable channelling and tunnelling through the Wolds chalk.

The footpath follows the old line eastwards until the Wolds Way sign points up some steps cut in the steep embankment on the left. Ahead is a bridge (not on the Wolds Way) before the two-kilometre Drewton Tunnel which emerges just short of Little Weighton. It is now blocked off.

At the top, a well-defined path leads away from the line into West Hill Plantation towards Hunsley Dale and East Dale. Bear left at a fork into the prettiest dell you will see on this walk. Watch out for families of long-tailed tits. The path narrows as it rises to the head of East Dale, passing several historic boundary stones, and emerges at a stile into a field. Turn left and follow the field round to the busy B1230. The mast is Hunsley Beacon, which transmits radio programmes to the area.

Go almost straight across and follow the field division round to the right until it emerges on another road. Turn right and go straight on at the junction. Almost everything around is cultivated. At a plantation on the right, the Wolds Way leaves the road along a field boundary on the left (normally a track but sometimes ploughed) and follows it down the hill, swinging round to the right with the first hedge and continuing to a stile which is crossed to go down into the dale. Follow the dale bottom on a barely distinct track which leads through a gate and proceeds west down the peaceful Swin Dale. Look for pied and grey wagtails at the dew-pond, unusual in that it is concrete rather than clay-lined.

A left fork climbs out of the dale after a while, leading to the village of North Newbald. Wolds Way walkers, though, go straight on. The metalled road at the end of Swin Dale provides another opportunity to go into the village, which has refreshment facilities including two pubs (the Gnu and the Tiger) and is best known for its church, dating from the twelfth century and certainly among the most superb examples of Norman church architecture in the country. To

Goodmanham

rejoin the route, take the Beverley road from the village
green, then the first turning left which is followed round
leftward until the farm track is reached. Turn up this track
(where there may still be a Wolds Way sign as this was the
original route) and follow the path to rejoin the Wolds Way at
Hessleskew Gare.

Those not visiting Newbald should turn right on the road
and then left on a track immediately past a farm. The track
past the farm leads to another road where you turn right and
then after a while left on an almost dead-straight two-
kilometre track over the hill to another metalled road.
Follow the road straight ahead, past the large Hessleskew
farm, and cross the main Beverley-to-York road with care.
Again, the view is still unvaried, every field under the
plough and every verge a riot of white deadnettle and cow
parsley in summer. Immediately across the road, branch left
towards Arras, a farm whose name is best known for the late
Iron Age burial ground nearby. Kipling Cotes Racecourse
can be reached from here by carrying straight on (see page
55). The cemetery, a short distance along the main road
towards Market Weighton, was found to contain a wealth of
relics of Parisii warriors. Chariots, horse-harnesses and the
skeletons of ponies were found as well as bronze brooches,
armlets and beads. A reconstruction of a Parisii burial is one
of the displays at the Transport and Archaeology Museum in
Hull's old High Street. There are also exhibits in the British
Museum in London.

Go through the farm, keeping most of the buildings on your
left and then go round the back and out of the back gate,

ignoring the track curving up round the farm. Join a ragged hedgerow ahead and keep it on the right, walking north-west in an almost straight line. At a clump of elder and hawthorn, which almost blocks the way, a path leads through with another hedge and broken fence. Finally, come down a slight incline past a small plantation and over a stile to descend into the spillway of Market Weighton Gap. This natural valley carried the railway line from the town to Beverley. It opened in 1865 but was one of the victims of Beeching's cuts and closed in November 1965. It is now a bridleway.

Continue straight ahead on the metalled lane leading down to the 'Gate' sign. The railway line's course is now clearly visible and a bridge once carried it across this road. The village of Goodmanham is a little over one kilometre farther up the road.

Just round the corner from the railway line, you pass Rifle Butts Quarry, the Yorkshire Naturalists' Trust reserve (not open to the public). It offers refuge to willow warblers and ringlet and common butterflies. Its chief point of interest, however, is its unusual section of red and white chalks.

The Market Weighton alternative

7 kilometres

The obvious way to approach Market Weighton is by the old railway line. The tracks have long since been torn up and the signals removed, but nothing else has changed. The steep embankments are piled with hawthorn for most of the two kilometres into town, providing huge feasts in autumn for redwings, fieldfares, blackbirds and thrushes. When the first houses are reached, another old railway line, linking Market Weighton with Driffield, swings in from the right. It opened in April 1890, mainly as a link in a proposed connection of the Hull-Barnsley line to Scarborough, but the southerly section to Howden was never built and the line's main function was to carry West Riding people to the coast in summer. It was finally closed by Beeching in August 1965. Past some new houses, turn left at the road to reach the main street.

Market Weighton is an old-fashioned market town, its main street lying on a turnpike and later developments spreading to the rear of the largely eighteenth-century buildings. Next to the Methodist Church on the west side of the town is a smaller building where Wesley once preached. The parish church of All Saints, the clock tower of which is a prominent landmark, has in its graveyard the remains of William Bradley, a giant who died in 1820 at the age of 33. Towering 7 ft 9 in high and weighing 27 stones, Bradley made his name around the fairgrounds of the country as a freakshow attraction. He is still named in the record books as England's tallest man.

To rejoin the Wolds Way, take the York road out of town and find a stile on the right immediately past the pig farm. An indistinct path cuts across a field reclaimed from the Market Weighton-to-York railway line, which carried its last train on the same day in 1965 as did the line from the town to Beverley. Make for the left-hand end of a hedgerow running on the other side of the field for the start of over one kilometre of rather monotonous walking along the sides of five fields, passing from one to the other by way of timber

Mᵣ Wᵐ BRADLEY.

In the Year 1792.

William Bradley, England's tallest man, 1792–1820

(*Photograph of the engraving by kind permission of the Londesborough Arms, Market Weighton*)

planks across drainage ditches.

Cross the main road, go past Towthorpe Farm, through a gate into a field and follow the distinct track which curves round with the trees to emerge on another road. Turn left and then right through the tall wrought-iron gates of Londesborough Park, passing the gate lodge and follow the estate road up to join the Wolds Way where another track snakes up the hill from the right.

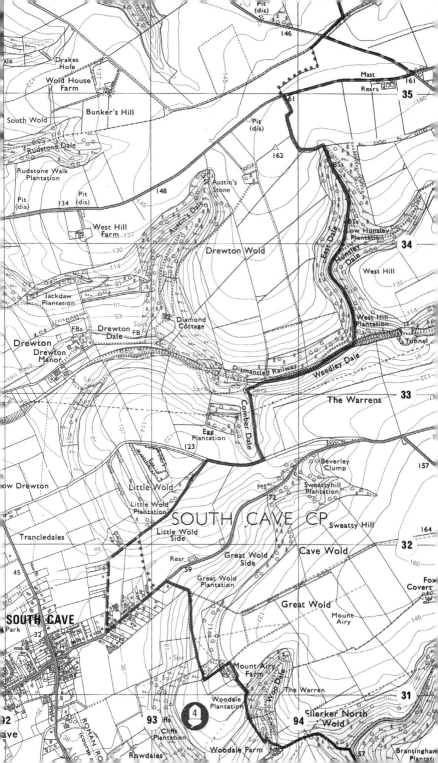

Goodmanham to Thixendale

32 kilometres

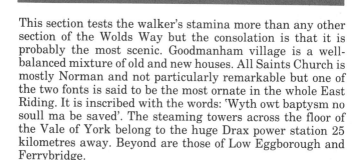

This section tests the walker's stamina more than any other section of the Wolds Way but the consolation is that it is probably the most scenic. Goodmanham village is a well-balanced mixture of old and new houses. All Saints Church is mostly Norman and not particularly remarkable but one of the two fonts is said to be the most ornate in the whole East Riding. It is inscribed with the words: 'Wyth owt baptysm no soull ma be saved'. The steaming towers across the floor of the Vale of York belong to the huge Drax power station 25 kilometres away. Beyond are those of Low Eggborough and Ferrybridge.

Leave the village between the church and Brook Farm. Down the hill and under the bridge that once carried the Market Weighton-to-Driffield railway line the path bends round to the left and into a field, continuing round the side and emerging at a large picnic area on the A163 (busy in summer with holiday traffic from South Yorkshire to Bridlington).

A few kilometres to the north-east is one of the most curious features, not, unfortunately, touched by the path – the Kipling Cotes Racecourse. This is the home of the Kipling Cotes Derby, which was started in 1519 and is the oldest horse-race in England. It is still run every year on the third Thursday in March. The course can be inspected by making a detour up the A163 and turning right at the first small crossroads. The start is best reached from Arras (see page 46).

Crossing the main road, the path continues straight ahead along the side of a field. This is the course of an old Roman road which ran from Malton to Brough. It meets a metalled road and proceeds towards the Londesborough Estate, which is pleasantly set out ahead. Fork left at a gate beneath a circle of six chestnut trees and follow the track cut into the grass across a field, curving down to a gate by the bottom of the conifer plantation to a plank bridge.

The stream it crosses flows into an artificially created lake

which formed part of the great Londesborough Park laid out by the third Earl of Burlington in the eighteenth century. The village of Londesborough was occupied as early as Roman times and was also reputed to be the site of a summer palace for the Kings of Northumbria. The present estate began to take shape in the fifteenth century but when it passed to the Cavendishes, the sixth Duke of Devonshire demolished the house in 1819 and much of the material was taken for new buildings at Chatsworth. Even without the Hall, the Londesborough Estate still remains exceptionally beautiful. One of the most interesting features is a superb avenue of elms planted in memory of the great actor, David Garrick, who was a friend of the third Earl and a regular visitor to the estate. Londesborough's most famous owner, however, was the railway king George Hudson, who bought the 4,850-hectare estate for £470,000 in 1845 and then ran his York-to-Market Weighton line to a specially built private station near the estate. Hudson's grand style of living did not last long, however, because his business empire collapsed in 1849.

Ahead of you at the foot-bridge is the red-brick Londesborough Hall of today. To the left are some remains of the old hall, mainly a stepped terrace and some urns on pedestals. The avenue of trees is followed up the gentle slope and then down into a dip and round to a junction of tracks (this is where the Wolds Way is rejoined by walkers who choose to visit Market Weighton).

Follow the track up the hill, through the gate and round to your left. Go straight up the hill through the wood to the road, then swing to the left after passing Londesborough School, walking on to turn right at the 'Give Way' sign. Now begins 1.5 kilometres of road-walking but the lane is usually quiet as it is chiefly a link between two minor roads. The views are interesting since the road goes right along the fringe of the Wolds. At the T-junction turn right and then left over the cattle grid into Partridge Hall. Go through the farmyard and out through the orchard at the rear to a track which leads to Thorns Wood.

Above rises Burnby Wold. Past the wood, you are confronted with the picturesque village of Nunburnholme in the dale below. To reach it, cross a stile and continue with the fence to your right, then down at the corner to a foot-bridge and stile at the bottom. Small boys fishing with worms on hooks in Nunburnholme Beck say there are trout big enough to eat here. Across the field is a stile on to the main village street.

The village is strung along one road and is named after a priory of Benedictine nuns, founded in the twelfth century. Nothing of that remains. All around the red roofs and white walls of the cottages is some of the richest greenery to be seen in the Wolds. In spring and summer the dale has a constant chorus of bird-song, so it is little wonder that the village

e old railway
e near
odmanham

ndesborough
ll

Anglo-Saxon cross at Nunburnholme Church

produced an ornithologist of note – the Rev. Francis Orpen
Morris, rector of Nunburnholme between 1854 and 1893.
Morris was greatly influenced by the writings of that great
eighteenth-century naturalist and curate, Gilbert White, and
between 1851 and 1857 published his own six-volume *A
History of British Birds*. The church bell is inscribed: 'I will
imitate your birds by singing'. Most people, however, visit
the church to see the fine Anglo-Saxon cross dating from
1000. Among the carvings on the shaft are a madonna and
child and some animals.

The Wolds Way turns left on the road just past the church
and then right up two sides of a field to another road. Go up
the hill and then fork right on the track disappearing into the
deciduous Bratt Wood. This is one of the steepest inclines yet,
but the path soon becomes less severe as it leads into a field,
past Hessey Barn, on towards the top corner – and a stile –
across the field ahead. The path becomes a clear farm track
through Wold Farm, where you turn left before the buildings,
and on the other side becomes a metalled lane. Turn right
just before the solitary house, go to the top of the field and

turn left by a gate, then along the field edge. The path leads across the road connecting the village of Warter with Pocklington. Go straight over to the stile and across the field in front at an angle, to the top corner of a wood.

From here, walk along the side of the hill, keeping the fence on your left and turn right by a hand-gate standing on its own, up the side of a field to a track which leads through Warrendale House Farm. Over in the distance to the left, from several points along this section, it is possible to pick out the mighty bulk of York Minster, standing well clear of the rest of the city's roof-tops 25 kilometres away.

Past the farm, a road zig-zags in and out of Warrendale to a junction. If your accommodation is in Pocklington, turn left here and follow the road for over a kilometre until you come to a footpath sign on the right which brings you eventually on to the main road just east of the town. Rejoin the path by the same route. Continue up the track and follow the side of Warrendale Plantation to the top of the hill, leaving behind the fringe of the Wolds which you have followed since Market Weighton. Now the path cuts into the Wolds where skylarks and sheep are the walker's constant companions.

Bratt Wood

Don't go through the gate at the top, but bear left and follow the fence over the slight rise towards the gateposts ahead. Turn left down a slope for a short distance, then swing right and walk between a fence and a line of fence-posts. Below is the village of Millington. A stile on the left in the hedge leads down to the village. Farther on to the right is Millington Pasture, which in summer is a favourite haunt of ramblers, naturalists and picnic parties. The pasture looks essentially as much of the Wolds looked before the agricultural revolution. The main field had over 162 hectares and was shared by the farmers in the district. Each rented a number of 'gaits' or 'stints', the names given to a section in which six sheep or four ewes and their lambs could be grazed. There were 108 gaits but all this ended in the 1960s when the pasture was enclosed and mostly cultivated. Despite this, the view of Millington Pasture across from the Wolds Way is truly glorious. There was a huge public outcry at the time of the enclosure, ramblers organised mass rambles, and paths were eventually agreed. The fate of the pastures serves as a reminder that no section of countryside, however popular, remains safe from change.

Past Warren Farm, the Way bears right and then proceeds along the brow of the hill again, following the course of an old earthworks. It descends gradually to a dale known as Rabbit Warren, though there are few rabbits to be seen. The name is a relic from the seventeenth and eighteenth centuries when many farmers encouraged the breeding of rabbits for their meat and fur.

At the bottom the way ahead is painfully clear – up the steep incline to the top of the hill, keeping trees and bushes on the left. This helps seasoned long-distance footpath walkers rediscover their calf muscles. Others will take it at an easier pace. Once at the top, continue as before and then drop down again, this time into Nettle Dale where nettles are only slightly less thin on the ground than were rabbits in the previous dale. But cowslips are numerous. Again, the path shoots up the steep side of the dale, but this time turns off to the right near the top, towards Jessops Plantation. Go over a stile and through two gates and turn sharp left at the end of the trees. Once out of the wood turn right and follow the top of Huggate Sheepwalk, which emerges on a road. At a junction, go straight across the stile between two white gates and climb gently to what is – at just under 200 metres above sea-level – one of the highest points on the Wolds Way. Apparently a farmer once put a trailer of hay in this field and stood on it to see how far the view stretched. He saw Sheffield and Hull and the towers of Lincoln Cathedral and York Minster. At night he could see the beam of Flamborough Lighthouse to the east.

Turn right on the track and follow it across the road and past Glebe Farm. To the north-east is a wood shaped like a diamond. It was planted with larch for Queen Victoria's

View from the escarpment near Millington

Diamond Jubilee, but the larches were cut down for pit props in the Second World War, and a mixture of trees, bushes and weeds grew up in their place, still forming the same diamond shape on the landscape.

The track passes Glebe Farm and emerges on a metalled lane just north of Huggate. The village is one of the highest in the Wolds and suffers badly from snow-drifts in the winter. Houses and farm buildings are arranged round a large village green which has a deep well. The fourteenth-century tower of St. Mary's Church has battlements. Huggate has a post-office-shop and the Wolds Inn, which provides accommodation and meals. Many yellow arrows on gateposts around the village should not confuse Wolds Way walkers – they relate to a series of short circular walks round the district. (Leaflets are available from Humberside County Council.)

Turn left on the lane and follow the road past some very large fields. This landscape is mainly denuded of hedgerows and small groups of trees as it is intensively farmed. The Wolds Way takes a field-side path to the left of the road and descends into Horse Dale at an angle to the right, proceeding northwards up lonely Holm Dale, where you may be lucky

Holm Dale

enough to see orange-tip butterflies which are numerous
near the sheepfolds in summer. Holm village, now disappeared, was one of the many medieval villages depopu-
lated by the Black Death or changes in farming practice.
There are numerous earthworks left.

The path rises to the head of the dale. Go over the stile
under two large chestnut trees and take the track into
Fridaythorpe, turning right on the main street. The village is
yet another mixture of old and new, the old buildings mostly
red-brick and functional and not particularly quaint. There
are two ponds, which is unusual for villages in chalkland, but
they were probably created artificially with saucers of clay.
The simple church is mostly Norman and is another of the
restorations for the second Sir Tatton Sykes of Sledmere.
Those wishing to visit Sledmere (see Places of Interest, page
101) can get the Bridlington bus to the village from
Fridaythorpe.

Turn left off the main street and take the road signposted
'Thixendale', passing the pond. Before reaching the last farm,
a track shoots off to the left through a succession of fields
before dipping down into West Dale. Go up the other side,
keeping Ings Plantation on the left. Here, in the ash trees, is
a substantial rookery. The track goes right to the top but just
at the point at which it joins a hedge, strike up the grassy
slope to your right. At first, the path is indistinct but over the
top you should aim for a signpost and stile which can be seen
across the field between two telegraph poles.

Here the path becomes a clear farm track to Gill's Farm,
surrounded by trees. Turn right at the metalled lane and
then left before a house to begin one of the most pleasant
sections of the entire route. The track curves round to the
left, past a dew-pond and down, then doubles back northwards along the bottom alongside a splendid parade of

sycamore trees. The path to Thixendale is sinuous but easily followed. Rising steeply all around are uncultivated grazing grounds, with nettles, cow parsley and cowslips struggling against one another for the light. Yellowhammers are numerous in the summer and there is often the cry of curlews. The track emerges on a metalled lane which leads to the village of Thixendale, nestling snugly between some of the steepest of valley sides. As you enter the village, the steep path at the other end, which you will take to start the next section, is prominently in view.

Near Warren Farm

Wolds Inn, Huggate

Gill's Farm

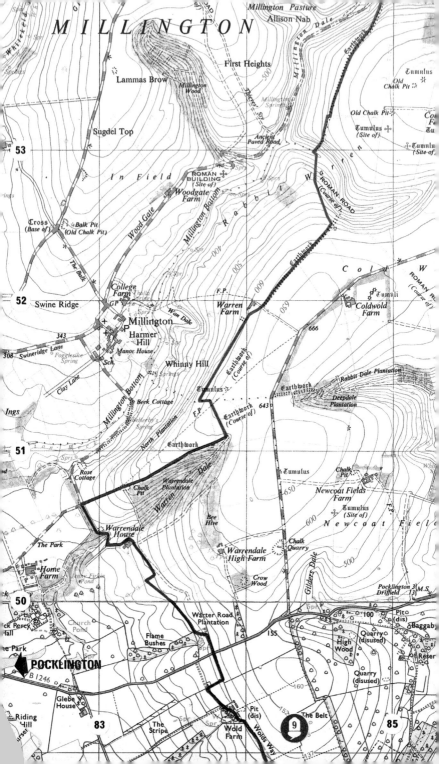

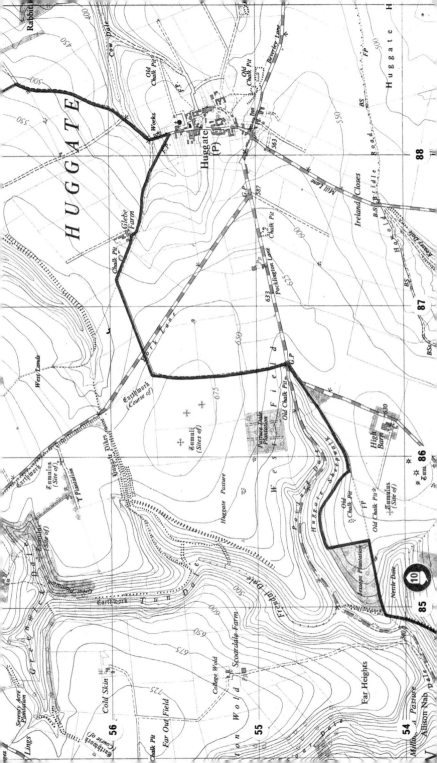

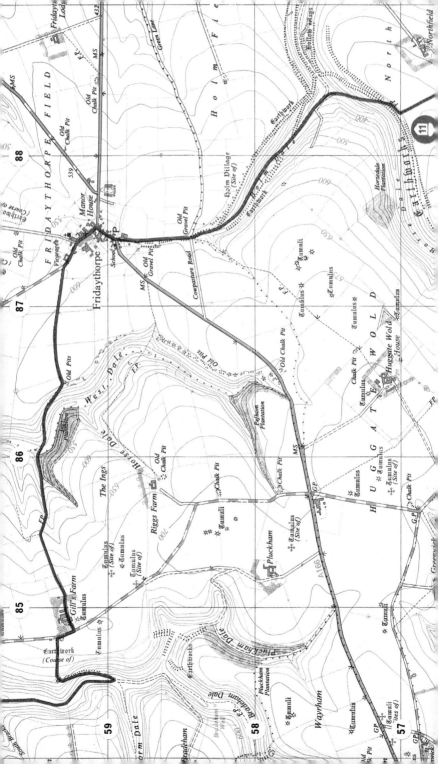

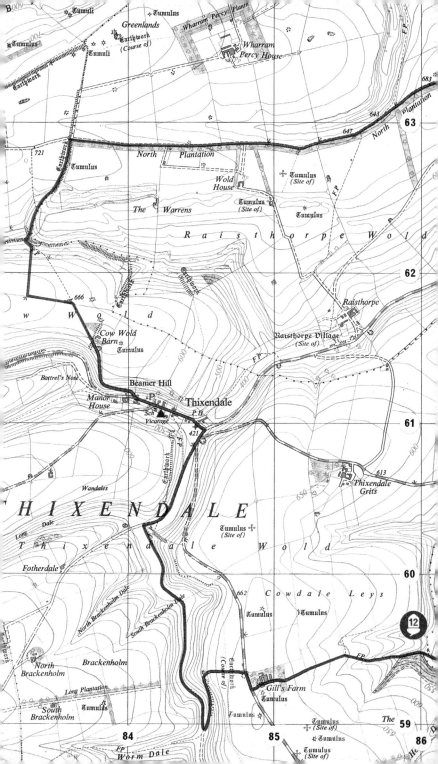

Thixendale to Sherburn

31 kilometres

Thixendale has the most remote and pastoral setting of any village in the Wolds, lying as it does at the bottom of steep-sided dales. Ploughed fields are few and in spring and summer the whole valley is alive with the constant bleating of lambs and sheep, which appear everywhere. At weekends the village is also busy with day trippers, usually *en route* to the coast.

There are two theories as to how Thixendale got its name. One is that it is so called because six dales meet there; the other, that it is because it is possible to count *sixteen* dales feeding Thixendale. The youth hostel reflects the changing priorities of the village. Built as a school by G.E. Street for the second Sir Tatton Sykes of Sledmere, it then became a village hall. It still has this role in the winter months, but in spring and summer it is full of bunk beds to cater for the cyclists and ramblers who naturally include Thixendale in their itineraries of the Wolds.

This section of the Wolds Way passes through very quiet country where hardly another soul is met. Features of historical interest are few, apart from Wharram Percy (not actually on the Wolds Way), but for most of the walk you will constantly be admiring the grand views of the Vale of Pickering and the southern edge of the North York Moors. In places the footpath becomes rather complicated as it zig-zags across agricultural land and it is essential to follow the map closely to prevent damage to crops. Follow the waymarks.

Leave Thixendale by the north road and opposite the farm go through a gate and up the hillside on a track, passing Cow Wold Barn on your right. Go over a stile and, keeping the field on the left, follow a track which crosses a stile and swings left along the edge of a field, keeping the fence on the left. Turn right and follow the field perimeter. All around is a highly cultivated landscape with hardly a building in sight.

The path descends gently to a dale. Look for a stile on the left taking you into the next field to reach the bottom, where Vessey Pasture Dale and Back Dale meet, then go up the

Burdale Quarry

other side beside a fence. This section continues up a gully to the corner of North Plantation, at which you should turn right on a grass track to begin a long section stretching for over three kilometres along the Wold side, gradually curving left. Along the path are some very wide fields demonstrating how prairie-like modern farming methods can make a landscape, though the wide view northwards of Wharram Percy Farm is no small compensation. The hedges that have been left have been allowed to grow tall and thick.

After a couple of kilometres a dale shoots away to the north, leading to the deserted medieval village of Wharram Percy (see Places of Interest, page 103). Continue on to Tunnel Plantation, so named because below it runs the Burdale railway tunnel, which is almost two kilometres long and took six years to construct before the Malton-to-Driffield line was opened in 1853. The link served two purposes: firstly, to get out thousands of tonnes of chalk which were quarried in the district, particularly near Wharram Percy; and secondly, to help farmers get their produce to the market towns at either end. The last train used the line in 1958 and the only trace of the tunnel at the wood is an air vent.

Pass the wood and join the metalled road, turning left towards Bella House with fine views ahead. The red roofs of Malton can clearly be seen to the north-west. Just before the farm is the public access track to Wharram Percy, which is one kilometre away down the track into the dale. Most walkers will probably want to visit this village site. The Wolds Way does not pass it because it was thought that too much disturbance might be detrimental to the ancient monument and so walkers are left to make up their own minds about the value of a visit.

Leave the road at a sharp right-hand bend, crossing a stile to a path towards a group of houses. Turn right on the road into Wharram le Street. The village church has Anglo-Saxon and Norman features but otherwise there is nothing of note here. The school, dated 1871, has – like so many village schools – ceased to be a centre of education and is now the hub of social activities, the village hall. The road straight on at the crossroads leads to Duggleby and the largest known neolithic barrow in Britain.

Turn left at the main road and, just past the last houses on the left, take a public bridleway on the right leading up the wold hillside. Keep straight on over a metalled road on to a farm track. At a barn look for a gap in the hedge to your left and go round the field corner, keeping to the hedge side for some 250 metres until there is a stile in the hedge. Use the well-constructed stile and continue west for a short distance and then down the hill to a foot-bridge crossing Whitestone Beck. Go up the hill under the large oak tree and turn right on to a track which winds past Settrington Wood House to meet Settrington Wood. Here, you branch round to the right along the side of the plantation and take another right fork 30 metres on, following the trees on the left. Screed Wood, as it is called, is mainly sycamore with some beech and ash. In spring and summer it is full of pink campion. Turn left at Wold Barn to continue straight on, with the wood this time to the right. Walk to the road and cross over into the wood by Beacon Wold, a service reservoir for a borehole into the chalk

Stubble burning above Thixendale

Vale of Pickering

below. On the left through the gate is an OS trig point. Here you are 198 metres above sea-level.

The path through this wood is delightful on a hot day, the density of the plantation allowing just a cool shaded passage. Curve right and then left down a tunnel-like path to the daylight streaming in through the exit ahead. At the gate is probably the most panoramic view to be had on the entire walk, part of its attraction being that it is so unexpected.

The Wolds escarpment falls away to flat farmlands. Malton is much closer than before; the Vale of Pickering is a patchwork of fields; and the North York Moors spread out across the entire northern aspect, while below there is the village of Wintringham, your next objective.

Go over the stile and down to the left in the entrenchment, then straight on, joining a metalled road across the floor of the dale for almost two kilometres. The road is very quiet as it leads only to Rowgate Farm. Just past a small reservoir, where a spring is trapped, find a public bridleway on the right (continue straight on for the village of Rillington) leading along the side of one field and across another to a gate and a foot-bridge over Wintringham Beck. Walk to the main road and turn left. The village lies to the right and, although its low whitewashed houses are attractive, there is little point in exploring because there are no shops or refreshments available. There is only a post office, which is just that.

Past a crescent of houses, turn sharp right along what is known locally as Back Side, a bridleway running the full length of the village. The church at the end is one of the largest in the area and has many interesting features. A series of saints' portraits can be seen on the aisle windows, with inscriptions that are probably sixteenth century. The white glass is stained yellow, which experts say is highly

unusual outside the City of York. Bellringers are instructed
by an inscription on the tower's inner wall:

'I pray you Gentlemen beware
And when you ring ye Bells take care;
For he that Rings and breaks a stay,
Must pay Sixpence without delay.
And if you ring in Spurs or Hatt
You must likewise pay Sixpence for that.
    – Michael Gill, Clerk, 1723.'

Just past the church, turn left up the hill towards the
woods. This is the start of almost 100 metres of ascent. Go
over a stile and turn left on the forest track. This plantation
was started in the late nineteenth century and is one of the
most extensive forests in the Wolds. At the end of a long
straight section up the hill, turn sharp right through a gap in
the trees to begin the severest incline of all on the Wolds
Way. It comes out at a stile into a field. While you recover
your breath, examine the North York Moors, which are now
very close indeed. Go straight on along the course of an old
earthworks. The right turn at the far end is also the main
swing eastwards of the footpath after it has run an almost
constant south-north direction.

Pass West Farm to a stile by a white gate on the left and at
the bridlegate turn right on to a pleasant track lined with
rowan, beech and hawthorn. The walk proceeds along West
Heslerton Brow, a peaceful green terrace, and keeps straight
on when the main track angles down the hill. Rabbits are
everywhere here, and so are stinging nettles. If you are lucky
you will find some wild rhubarb. From this general area, on a
clear day, you should be able to catch your first proper view of
the sea.

Turn right at the field corner and continue inside the field.

Cross the road to a track which leads eastwards past a plantation of conifers. Take a sharp left turn down behind the trees and then a right-hand turn, following the path eastwards, with a fence on the left. Below is the village of West Heslerton and farther on is East Heslerton, with its distinctive church built by Street in 1877 for the second Sir Tatton Sykes.

At the end of this long field, cross the stile and turn down to the bottom of another field, over a stile and then bear right along the lower side of the fence to the small wood next to Manor Wold Farm. Round the trees to a farm road, turn down to the left and then to the right into a field and continue east again for almost one kilometre. Eventually, you will see a signpost pointing down a faint track that acts as a division between two crops. At the far end turn seawards again along the side of the hill. At the top corner of Crowsdale Wood cut back up the hill and turn left on to the metalled lane.

From here it is a simple walk down to Sherburn. The lane is steep, twisting and narrow in places and, for road safety as much as for enjoyment, the path is taken off the hard surface and along the side of a field on the right for about 400 metres before emerging again on the road. On the straight stretch into the village, a track through the field on the right continues the walk to Ganton, but weary walkers will make the short detour into Sherburn, which has accommodation and refreshments waiting.

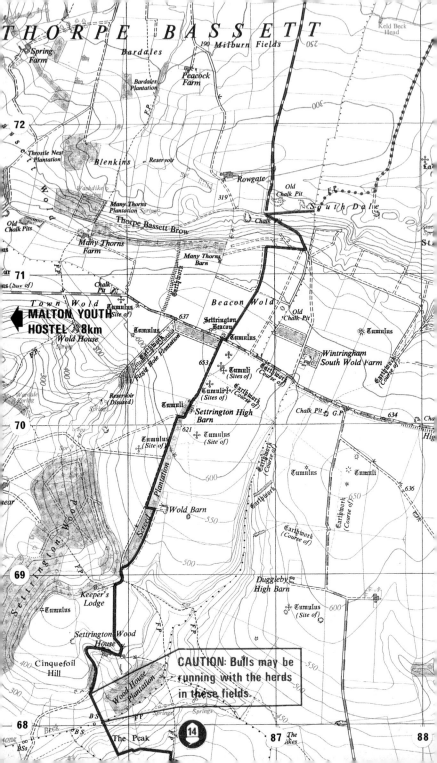

Sherburn to Filey

28 kilometres

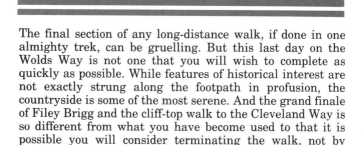

The final section of any long-distance walk, if done in one almighty trek, can be gruelling. But this last day on the Wolds Way is not one that you will wish to complete as quickly as possible. While features of historical interest are not exactly strung along the footpath in profusion, the countryside is some of the most serene. And the grand finale of Filey Brigg and the cliff-top walk to the Cleveland Way is so different from what you have become used to that it is possible you will consider terminating the walk, not by retracing steps into Filey but by continuing along the Cleveland Way into Scarborough.

Sherburn is for many people in Yorkshire no more than a name-plate on the A64 to Scarborough or the place with that pub with the unusual name, The Pigeon Pie. The church of St. Hilda has a Norman tower with interesting Saxon sculptures inside.

Those stopping at Sherburn should rejoin the path by going back up the lane from the main road. Pedants will take the right fork and turn left on to the track through a field, thereby not missing an inch of the Wolds Way. Others will go left, straight up the metalled lane which leads to Butterwick, Foxholes and Weaverthorpe. Pass High Mill on your left. According to a datestone, the main building was constructed in 1843. A spring rising at the foot of the Wolds was dammed to make a mill-pond, now a favourite place for wildfowl and swans. Some of the old mill machinery is still there but electricity is now used to make animal feeds. The long pond is surrounded by superb mature poplars, seen as you walk up the road.

Take the offshoot signposted to Foxholes but look for a stile and a path on the left leading up the side of the field alongside a thick hedge. This curves up the hill to a gate into a small plantation. Ahead, temptingly, is a good view of the cliffs above Filey Brigg and the end of the Wolds Way.

The path becomes a clear grass track through the trees and in summer it is difficult to avoid trampling on the forget-me-

Skylark

Yellow
hammer

Corn
bunting

Weasel

Cow
parsley

Pink   Long-tailed Greater   Harebell
campion   fieldmouse   stitchwort
                                   Scarlet pimpernel

nots and buttercups. Below the trees are celandines and
cowslips. Just when you are settling down to an unhurried
woodland stroll, the path leads off the track to a hand-gate
into a field. This takes you back down the slope of the
northern escarpment of the Wolds and you lose the height
you had gained. The Way soon turns eastwards again on a
farm track. Pass a small conifer wood, aim slightly to the left
of a large barn and turn right at the lane. Take a sharp left
turn on to a track, go over a stile and proceed eastwards to
another lane. Turn left here and then right, within sight of a
magnificent copper beech. This is the village of Ganton,
where refreshments and accommodation are available down
by the main road.

Up to the right is Ganton Hall, something of a Victorian French château in style, set in sumptuous grounds. Up the Wolds escarpment is the site of an Anglian cemetery.

Go along Main Street past a new development and continue straight on at the left-hand bend. Keep the old stables to your left and hug the side of the vicarage garden to reach a field next to St. Nicholas Church, which has a particularly fine spire dating from the late fourteenth century. Continue north-eastwards along the top of the field, passing a line of chestnut trees, and through the plantation ahead, turning up its north-eastern side to where the trees end. Below are wide views of the coastal plain known as The Carrs, which reaches to Filey Bay. During the Ice Age this whole vale was under Lake Pickering, which was 40 kilometres long and nearly 13 kilometres wide. Over to the north-east the red roofs belong to Seamer and the outskirts of Scarborough.

Continue up for one more field, then turn north-eastwards and then south-eastwards when you reach a sunken lane called Wold Lane, which rises up the hillside. Pass an old

Staxton Wold

Larch   Wren   Sparrowhawk

chalk pit and continue on the lane, passing through one gate, then left at the next. Follow the hedge and cross a stile in it near the end. Continue along the field-boundary straight ahead, then through a stile in the hedge on the left. Follow the field edge to the road opposite Grange Farm. Staxton Brow picnic site, which has panoramic views, is half a kilometre away down the road to the left.

Cross the road but do not be deterred by the sign saying 'Private Road'. This leads up to RAF Staxton Wold, which is officially described as a 'radar air defence' station. It is one of a chain of early warning stations along the east of Britain.

Radio masts, revolving scanners and dishes are behind double security fences fortified with Dannert wire, and the whole place is undoubtedly one of the most fascinating features to be found along the Wolds Way, perhaps because you rarely have an opportunity to get so close to an important defence establishment. For security reasons you are advised not to take any photographs nearby.

Staxton Wold was opened on 1 April 1939, just in time to make a sizeable contribution to monitoring the *Luftwaffe*. For example, on 10 February 1942, it picked up 30 'hostiles' 240 kilometres out in the North Sea, heading towards England. On 23 August that year, its sighting of two enemy

Beech

Tawny owl

Sycamore

Celandines

bombers over Norfolk led to their being shot down. The closest it ever came to being bombed itself was in December 1942, when a Halifax bomber on an operational flight passed over Staxton with its fuselage on fire. It jettisoned a load of incendiary bombs and a 1000 lb bomb into an adjacent field.

Approach the base and follow the road right. Continue straight on down past a farm, and as the slope flattens out, go left up the steep bank beside a fence and hedge. Once over the stile at the top, proceed eastwards back up to high Wolds country. Here begin more than two kilometres of straight walking along the sides of undulating fields. In season, look for greater stitchwort and scarlet pimpernel in the hedge banks.

Turn right on the road and a little later left to follow the northern fence of Raven Dale, which meets the long, winding Camp Dale at a round cattle pond. Keep to the left up Bording Dale, opposite, and follow the fence right round the top. Three-quarters of the way round take a stile left to follow the upper rim of Camp Dale as it winds south-eastwards for the best part of a kilometre before meeting a fence and turning downwards, to cross a stile into the next field. Follow the fence down, past the boarded-over well, and round left into Stocking Dale, which, after Camp Dale, is a positive

oasis of greenery. On the corner is the site of a deserted village, but hardly anything remains. The path is well defined and goes straight through the trees at the end, passing an old quarry and through some bushes and swings up the hill to join a farm track. Cross the road at Stockendale Farm and take the track ahead for one kilometre, looking for an inconspicuous stile on your right which leads to a path crossing a field to another stile in a gap in the hedge. From here, the walk down the side of the field is the gradual descent that leaves the Wolds escarpment behind for the last time. The path crosses a stile and meets the main road just on the fringe of Muston.

Turn right into the village and go along the main street. Muston is a mixture of eighteenth-century and Victorian white-fronted houses, mostly built along what is now the A1039. The church, passed on the left, was restored in 1863. Go round two left-hand bends. The footpath continues by the right of the terrace of houses immediately ahead, in a layby, across two small fields. Take care crossing the busy A165 main road between Bridlington and Scarborough. Ahead is a stile leading into a field and through a white hand-gate to a long narrow field called Thorn Balk. Walk down the right side of the field towards the roofs of Filey. Half-way down, the footpath goes in to the side with a fence on the left and school playing fields on the right, crosses a foot-bridge at the end and takes you on to a path leading to the main road.

As you walk down the road into Filey, and go over the level crossing, you will see all the features of a commercialised holiday resort. Yet Filey has somehow managed to retain the character of a small fishing town, which it still is, restraining the tourist amenities from taking over too much and restricting them as much as possible to only a few months of the year. To many people, Filey is the most idyllic spot on the whole of the east coast.

Camp Dale dewpond

ar
ston

Filey from the Brigg

Turn left at the Methodist Church into Union Street, and then right at the end. You join Mitford Street only briefly before turning left along Reynolds Street into Queen Street, which is one of the oldest streets in Filey and has for generations been the centre of the local fishing community. As you walk towards the sea you will pass a house with a model of a ship above the door. This is T'Awd Ship Inn, once a meeting place for smugglers. The benches at the end of Queen Street, overlooking the Bay, are often occupied by old fishermen who will tell you a story or two if you get into conversation with them.

Go down the steps to Coble Landing. This is a hub of activity in Filey throughout the year, but during the summer kiddies with buckets and spades mingle with fishermen in huge sea-boots. A board with some old brass clocks will tell you what the state of the tide is, in case you planned to walk back to Filey by the rocky shore path.

The Wolds Way continues up the rough path behind the entertainment and lifeboat buildings on the Landing. The path goes along Pampletine Cliffs, then down and back up a small dale past the local yachting club's dinghy park. The spongy turf is followed right out to the Brigg. There is a snack bar here in the summer. Descend with care the narrow path cut in the cliff-top to the reef, which is a wonderland for marine biologists. You will probably want to spend at least half an hour exploring the rock pools in search of shellfish, which are left by every tide.

Carr Naze, which is above the Brigg, was the site of a Roman signal station, but there is nothing left behind, although some pottery and coins have been found in the past.

Scarborough is seen clearly to the north, particularly the castle towering above the resort. The walk along the cliff to the end of the Wolds Way is exhilarating, even after a long-distance walk. Meadow pipits take the place of skylarks and down on the sea there are dashing fishing parties of guillemots, razorbills and puffins. The finish is as unremarkable as the start. You began at a pub car park and you wind up at a line of fence-posts, which was once the old East Riding county boundary. Here, also, ends the Cleveland Way.

Landing cobles at Filey

The Brigg, Filey

The Way near Muston Wold Farm

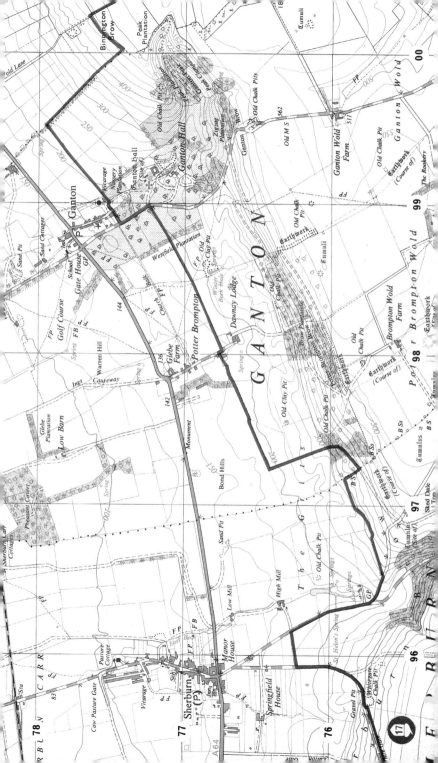

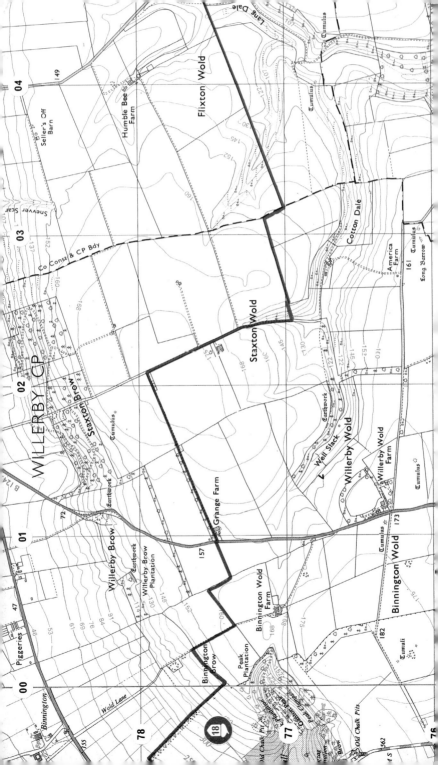

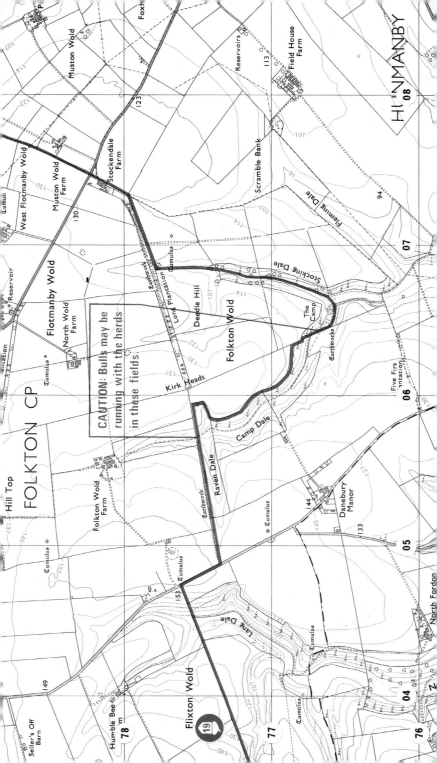

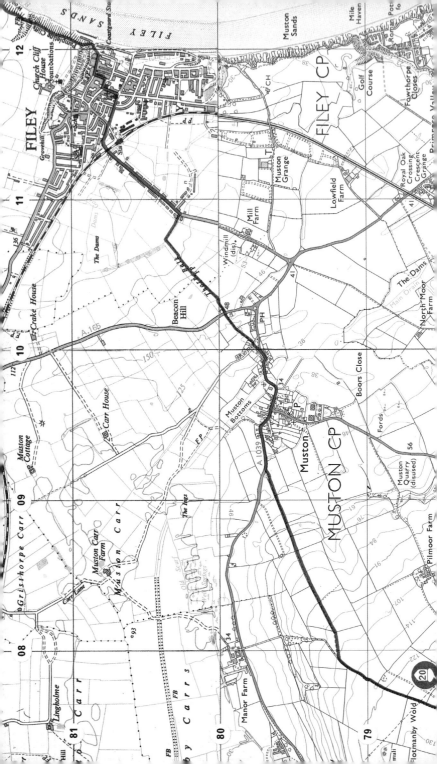

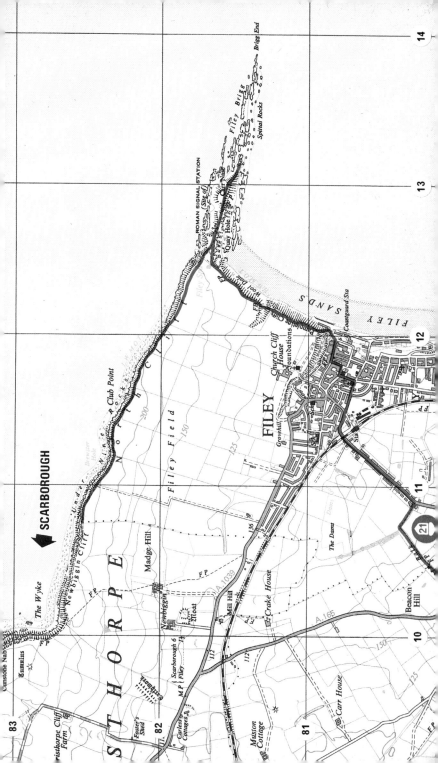

Nearby places of interest

Not every interesting feature in the Yorkshire Wolds is directly on the footpath. This is a brief gazetteer of towns, villages, country houses, scenic gems and assorted peculiarities within 20 kilometres or so of the Wolds Way.

Bempton

orth cliffs,
ley

A tiny village between Filey and Flamborough, more famous for its cliffs. The massive precipice is the home of huge numbers of seabirds and is a reserve belonging to the Royal Society for the Protection of Birds. Access is by the road running east from the pub and there is a car park and information hut. The best time of year to visit is late May to early July, when the adult bird population is swollen by thousands of chicks.

Beverley

An ancient market town dominated by its magnificent minster. Many of the streets have survived virtually unchanged from the eighteenth century and there are many individual buildings going back to medieval times. There are hundreds of hectares of common pasture-land on the fringes, making Beverley altogether one of the most attractive towns in the North. It was formerly the county town of the old East Riding and is now the base for many departments of Humberside County Council. Most visitors flock to the minster, which stands to one side of the town. It is the size of a cathedral and, indeed, its design is similar to that of Lincoln Cathedral. The building began around 1230 and took 250 years to complete.

Bridlington

A noisy holiday resort in summer, but a pleasant fishing town for the rest of the year. The Georgian Old Town and harbour area are well worth exploring. Sewerby Hall, on the road to Flamborough, has many mementoes of Amy Johnson, the pioneer airwoman who was born in Hull. Bayle Gate, at

le of Pickering

Bridlington Priory Church, houses a small museum.

Driffield
The 'capital' of the Wolds. It is the most important centre for shops and services in the area and owes its growth to the great strides in agricultural production of the nineteenth century. The Driffield Canal, constructed in the late eighteenth century to link the town with the River Hull and the Humber, enabled grain and other agricultural produce to reach industrial towns. Humber keels returned with coal, fertilisers and building materials. Later, the railway took most of the traffic. Today the town reflects its functional past, with mills and maltings and agricultural machinery suppliers. It is a pleasant place to explore.

Flamborough
The chalk headland is said to get its name from the flaming beacon that once burned here. Beacon Tower, an octagonal stone structure, was built in 1674 and still stands some three kilometres from the village. The beacon in operation today is the new lighthouse, built in 1806, just 200 metres from the 'old' one near the cliff edge. The whole coast, an abrupt end to the Wolds, is riddled with caves. There are also stacks with names like 'the King and Queen' and 'Adam and Eve'. North Landing is at the bottom of a steep track and is busy with the activity of fishermen.

Hull
Kingston upon Hull, to give the city its full name, is not on many tourist itineraries, which is a shame because there is much of interest here. The Town Docks Museum in Queen Victoria Square is worth an afternoon of anybody's time. It is full of relics from the port's whaling and fishing past. The birthplace of the slave emancipator, William Wilberforce, is at 23-4 High Street and is open to the public. Most of Hull was razed by the *Luftwaffe* but, fortunately, the most valuable architectural treasure – the Old Town – remained virtually intact. Most of it is seventeenth and eighteenth century but Ye Olde White Harte, in Silver Street, dates from the late sixteenth century and it was here that the first overt act of the English Civil War took place, when the citizens of the town locked the gates on Charles I. The entire docks region is fascinating. At Victoria Pier there is an interesting contrast between the old dock gates, crumbling away, and the tall concrete and steel guillotine of the River Hull Tidal Surge Barrier, which was completed in 1980 to stop the city being flooded. (Over 90 per cent of Hull is almost two metres below the highest recorded tide level and too often the Old Town became Kingston *UNDER* Hull!)

Malton
The main shopping centre for villagers on the north-west shoulder of the Wolds. A recent by-pass has brought new life to its streets, once ruined by the constant thunder of traffic

The tallest standing stone in the country, Rudston

from West Yorkshire to the coast. Situated on the River Derwent, Malton became an important trading town when the river was fully open to navigation. Now there is little movement on the waters and the stretch from the town to Kirkham is very pretty. Malton Museum is full of Roman relics.

Pickering
Not in the Wolds but well worth a visit at the end of the walk because of its well-preserved railway. The North York Moors Railway runs for 27 kilometres through the National Park. It is one of the world's earliest lines, built by George Stephenson in the 1830s as a link between the sea at Whitby and the market town of Pickering, hub of a large farming area. It was closed in 1965 and re-opened privately eight years later to provide one of the most scenic journeys by steam train anywhere. Details are available from the North York Moors National Park. Pickering also has a museum of rural life in Beckside, and a Norman castle. Nearby, at Kirby Misperton, is Flamingoland Zoo.

Rudston
This pleasant village on the Roman road from York to Bridlington derives its name from 'rood', meaning cross, and

'stone', which refers to the tallest standing stone in the country, towering eight metres, next to the church. It is thought that the monolith, believed to date from the Bronze Age, probably had a cross-head at one time. The stone is one huge block of gritstone, which does not occur in the area. It is likely, therefore, that it was dragged over 16 kilometres from the nearest gritstone outcrop at Cayton Bay, near Scarborough. That must have been a vast operation, since it is estimated that the stone is embedded in the ground for almost another seven metres. Winifred Holtby, the novelist, was born at nearby Rudston House in 1898 and her untimely death in 1935 shocked the entire area. She is buried in the churchyard.

Scarborough

There are two sides to Scarborough. One is the noisy holiday resort of amusement arcades, fish-and-chip cafés and 'kiss me quick' hats. The other is a feast of the Victorian and the Edwardian. Visitors were first attracted to the spa in the seventeenth century, but before that there was a Roman signal station on the cliff-top, which later became the site of a twelfth-century castle. Henry II is said to have launched Scarborough Fair, now immortalised in song, with the

Skidby Mill

command that people should sport and play provided that
there was 'nowt amiss'. In recent years there have been
revivals of both fair and spa.

Skidby Mill

Built in 1821, this is the last surviving example of a windmill
in the North East and experts rate it as the best remaining
tower mill in the country. The tar-black tower and shining
white cap and sails form a prominent landmark 10
kilometres south of Beverley. The mill has been restored to
full working order and visitors can buy fresh stone-ground
flour. A recent addition is a small museum of relics from the
days when such windmills were commonplace. Open between
May and September.

Sledmere

Ancestral home of the Sykes family, who turned the
Yorkshire Wolds from a mostly uncultivated landscape into
some of the best arable land in the country. The family
fortune came from wool in seventeenth-century Leeds.
Sledmere, a Tudor house, passed into the family by marriage.
The original building was demolished and in its place a
Queen Anne-style house was constructed. The enlargement,

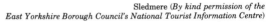

Sledmere (*By kind permission of the
East Yorkshire Borough Council's National Tourist Information Centre*)

in 1787, is what visitors come to see today: the design is by the pioneer agriculturalist, Sir Christopher Sykes, with help from Wyatt and the decorative plasterwork is by Joseph Rose, who worked with the Adam brothers. A fire in 1911 failed to destroy Rose's original drawings for the plasterwork and there is much else to see, including one interesting room decorated with Turkish tiles, and Chippendale, Sheraton and French furniture. Sir Christopher also brought in Capability Brown to design the gardens and park. His son, Sir Tatton, the fourth baronet, continued his great work in Wolds agriculture, and later the second Sir Tatton made his mark by bringing in the ecclesiastical architect G. E. Street both to restore and to build village churches throughout the Wolds. The village of Sledmere is six kilometres off the York-to-Driffield road and the house and grounds are open from Easter throughout the season.

Wharram Percy

A deserted medieval village and one of the most famous features of the Yorkshire Wolds, but avoided by the Wolds Way to save it from too much disturbance. The village site is only a short distance from the footpath and can be reached from Bella Farm, south of Wharram le Street. In common with many other villagers, Wharram Percy's inhabitants were virtually wiped out by the Black Death around 1350, but people were still living there as late as the early sixteenth century when, it is thought, the men who grew crops were simply made redundant because the farmers wanted the land for sheep to meet the increasing demand for wool. The cycle has turned full circle and the entire area surrounding the ruin, which is regularly excavated, is once more used for crops. The village has been described as 'the most promising of all village sites excavated in England', but there is little for the uninitiated to see. The church of St. Martin is the most obvious relic.

York

'The history of York is the history of England,' King George VI once said. York started as a temporary camp in the Roman campaign to defeat the Brigantes warriors in AD 71 and became an important garrison town. In the seventh century the Saxons arrived within its walls and built the first York Minster, of wood. It was in Norman times that York became England's second city. A great deal of its medieval architecture is well preserved: the superb minster, the city walls with embattled gateways, and the labyrinth of narrow streets and passages. Later centuries are well covered, and even re-created, in the fascinating Castle Museum, which has a superb model of a Victorian street. Britain's railway history is fully recorded at the Railway Museum.

Martin's Church,
harram Percy

103

Accommodation

Accommodation should not be a problem at the beginning and end of the Wolds Way. Hull, Hessle, North Ferriby and South Cave are long used to providing beds for visitors and, of course, Filey is a popular holiday resort with everything from self-catering flats to high-standard hotels.

But beds are less numerous in the Wolds themselves. Places offering bed and breakfast and evening meal on or close to the route are Goodmanham, Market Weighton, Huggate, North Grimston, Settrington, Thixendale, Rillington, Sherburn and Ganton. There is one, seasonal, youth hostel on the footpath, at Thixendale. It is simple grade and in the village hall, opposite the post office. The warden is the sub-postmistress (address: The Village Hall, Thixendale, Malton, North Yorkshire YO17 9TG. Tel. Driffield 88238). There is another simple-grade hostel, open mid-summer only, at Hull (Albemarle Youth Centre, Ferensway, Kingston upon Hull HU2 8LZ. Tel. Hull 20677). Further off the route, the youth hostel at Malton is open throughout the year (Derwent Bank, Malton, North Yorkshire YO17 0AX. Tel. Malton 2077). Further information on youth hostels is available from the Youth Hostels Association (see p. 107).

The East Yorkshire and Derwent Ramblers' Association has published an accommodation list in co-operation with the Countryside Commission. Many farms and private houses are expected to provide bed and breakfast once the Wolds Way becomes a well-known long-distance footpath.

The Ramblers' Association's *Bed and Breakfast Guide* is a useful source of information; also the English Tourist Board's *Where to Stay: Yorkshire and Humberside*.

There are no official camp sites along the Way but some farmers will allow tents to be pitched and will sell a few supplies. Perhaps a good idea is to look at the Ordnance Survey maps for the names of farms in the area you expect to spend a night, and then write to them (enclosing a stamped, addressed envelope) asking for permission to camp.

Iton Dale

Useful addresses

The Ramblers' Association
1-5 Wandsworth Road
London SW8 2LJ
Tel: 01-582 6878

Youth Hostels Association
Trevelyan House
8 St Stephen's Hill
St Albans
Hertfordshire AL1 2DY
Tel: St Albans 55215

Countryside Commission
Yorkshire and Humberside Regional Office
8A Otley Road,
Headingley
Leeds LS6 2AD
Tel: Leeds 742935/6

The Yorkshire Naturalists' Trust
20 Castlegate
York YO1 1RP
Tel: York 59570

Yorkshire and Humberside Tourist Board
312 Tadcaster Road
York YO2 2HF
Tel: York 707961

North York Moors National Park
The Old Vicarage
Bondgate
Helmsley
York YO6 5BP
Tel: Helmsley 70657

North Yorkshire County Council
County Hall
Northallerton
North Yorkshire DL7 8AH
Tel: Northallerton 3123

king west
north
s, Filey

Humberside County Council
Eastgate
Beverley
Humberside HU17 0DE
Tel: Hull 867131

British Railways Eastern Region
Regional Headquarters
York YO1 1HT
Tel: York 53022

East Yorkshire Motor Services
252 Anlaby Road
Hull HU3 2RS
Tel: Hull 27146/7

United Automobile Services Ltd
Feethams Bus Station
Feethams
Darlington DL1 5RA
Tel: Darlington 68771

Langdale from Flixton Wold

Reading list

The East Riding of Yorkshire Landscape by K. J. Allison. Hodder and Stoughton.
The East Riding by Geoffrey N. Wright. Batsford.
Yorkshire: York and the East Riding in 'The Buildings of England' series by Nikolaus Pevsner. Penguin.
The Humber by Anthony V. Watts. Lockington Publishing Co, North Ferriby.
Birds of the Yorkshire Coast by Richard Vaughan. Hendon.
The Agricultural Revolution in the East Riding of Yorkshire by Olga Wilkinson. East Yorkshire Local History Society. (This and many other interesting guides are available from the Society at Beverley Library, Champney Road, Beverley, North Humberside.)
Yorkshire, East Riding with York by Arthur Mee. Hodder and Stoughton.
The Sunday Times Book of the Countryside. Macdonald and Jane's.
A Field Guide to the British Countryside by A. Leutscher, ed. Sitwell. New English Library.
A Field Guide to the Birds of Britain and Europe by R. Peterson, G. Mountford and P. A. D. Hollom. Collins.
Birds of Sea and Coast by Lars Jonsson. Penguin.
Birds of Wood, Park and Garden by Lars Jonsson. Penguin.
Wild Flowers of Chalk and Limestone by J. E. Lousley. New Naturalist series. Collins.
The Concise British Flora in Colour by W. Keble Martin. Ebury Press and Michael Joseph.
British Trees in Colour by Cyril Hart and Charles Raymond. Michael Joseph.
A Field Guide to the Butterflies of Britain and Europe by L. G. Higgins and N. D. Riley. Collins.
The Observer Book of Wild Animals. Frederick Warne and Co Ltd.
Good Beach Guide by A. Smith and Jill Southam. Penguin.
British Regional Geology: Eastern England from the Tees to The Wash. Her Majesty's Stationery Office.

e old rail-
y cutting
Weedley
le

Enjoy the countryside and respect its life and work
Guard against all risk of fire
Fasten all gates
Keep your dogs under close control
Keep to public paths across farmland
Use gates and stiles to cross fences, hedges and walls
Leave livestock, crops and machinery alone
Take your litter home
Help to keep all water clean
Protect wildlife, plants and trees
Take special care on country roads
Make no unnecessary noise

Take care of the country

Hesslesk

Overleaf:
Staxton
Brow